Visitors to England

It is dangerous to dismiss the writings of contemporary observers. Whatever the accuracy of their work, it must be remembered that these people were actual witnesses to historical scenes and events. We are not. For centuries England was the focus of attention for a vast number of visitors sharing several common characteristics; they were not usually short of money and leisure and most of them were male and reasonably well educated.

Until the late eighteenth century these visitors frequently confined their curiosity to the south of England, with the great city of London acting as the magnet. At this time, many visitors travelled around England merely for the purposes of tourism and thus the wilder and more remote lands of the north were considered relatively unimportant. The few who did journey northwards usually centred their energies upon York. Foreign travellers in the medieval period were often wealthy aristocrats who devoted their time to visiting the various royal courts or religious centres such as the magnificent cathedral at Canterbury. A dominant theme with these early visitors was the famed beauty of English women. Nikolaus von Popplau, a member of a Silesian merchant family who visited the English court towards the end of the fifteenth century, held the opinion that English women "are like devils once their desires are roused, and when they take a fancy to someone whom they trust they grow quite blind and wild with love, more than the women of any other nation." The English as a nation, however, were not universally admired by their overseas guests. In 1465, a squire in the retinue of Leo of Rozmital in Bohemia delivered a scathing denunciation: "I have nothing more to record of the English, except that they are, as it seems to me, so cunning and treacherous that a foreigner cannot be sure of his life among them; however much they bend the knee, you cannot trust them."(1) One wonders what writers such as these would have made of Manchester!

The picturesque and apparently prosperous English countryside frequently elicited admiration, expressed typically in the writings of the German J W Archenholz. He has been criticised for his over-idealised portrayal of England, but others would have agreed with him when he wrote in 1785, "The whole country is full of parks which form beautiful views. All around one also sees fruit trees planted in avenues which lead to small villages where one meets country folk who are well-fed, well-dressed and enjoy a general prosperity which adequately shows the people's wealth, freedom and industry."(2) In a delightful essay in 1840, Friedrich Engels made another pleasing observation on this theme, to the effect that in England there is "no dazzlingly beautiful scenery, no colossal mountain masses, but a land of soft rolling hills which has a wonderful charm in the English sunlight... The trees, which occur singly or in groups in all the fields, have a singular beauty that makes the whole neighbourhood resemble a park." (3)

The means of travel for our intrepid visitors varied according to the period. Those who journeyed by coach had to face numerous problems such as highwaymen, bad weather, breakdowns and, most of all, the often appalling condition of the roads - especially in the north compl Lenss coach London in 1827, took exception to being confined in the same carriage with "four thieves in chains and a drunken woman." (4)

There were, of course, other modes of transport available. Some travellers, like Daniel Defoe and Celia Fiennis, chose to make their way on horseback, while others progressed at a more leisurely pace by making use of canal and river boats. After 1830, there were the railways which so often filled visitors with wonder. Engels spoke for many when he declared, "You who complain of the prosaic dullness of railways without ever having seen one should try travelling on the one from London to Liverpool. If ever a land was made to be traversed by railways it is England."(5) All these forms of travel have provided the means for visitors to experience and study the attractions of Manchester.

Visitors to Manchester

Before the mid-eighteenth century Manchester attracted few visitors who felt sufficiently inspired to commit their impressions of the town to paper. Those who did so were either antiquarians such as Leland, Camden, Stukeley and Horsley who endeavoured to record the few antiquities within the town, or travellers who were engaged upon an extensive tour of the country or region, and thus Manchester was only incidental to their enquiry.

Before the large scale industrialisation of Manchester, which took off in the late eighteenth century, the town was, by all accounts, a pleasant, populous and busy market town which largely owed its wealth to the woollen trade. Prior to the nineteenth century, most visitors noted and praised such familiar objects as the Collegiate Church (now the Cathedral), Chetham's College and Library, the Exchange, the Market Place and the other churches. These were seldom mentioned after 1800 because the rapid industrialisation of the town increasingly came to dominate the thoughts and pens of the visitors. There is, for instance, the work of the American writer Nathaniel Hawthorne, who in 1856 stated, "I had never visited Manchester before... neither is it particularly worth visiting, unless for the sake of its factories... it is a dingy, heavy town... built almost entirely within the present century."(6) This same point was more elaborately expressed by the Rev Richard Warner in 1800: "But the most remarkable feature in the character of Manchester is its trade, which, with a success hitherto unknown in the history of commerce, has

Nathaniel Hawthorne

spread itself all over the civilised world; and wafted the articles made at its manufactories from the ports of Britain to the most distant shores of both hemispheres... It is scarcely possible to conceive a more animated or curious scene than this work; where fifteen hundred people, young and old, are busily employed under one roof, directing the operations of machines of the most beautiful contrivance, which move with a rapidity that prevents the eye from detecting their rotations." (7)

Again before 1800, visitors to Manchester frequently praised the prosperity of the town and they sometimes favourably compared it with the old and wealthy centres of the woollen trade such as Norwich, the Cotswolds and York. These regions were eventually overtaken by the rising commercial dominance of Lancashire and West Yorkshire.

First impressions are often revealing and there are two accounts of Manchester which, even if only for their stark contrast, are particularly interesting. The first is by the previously-mentioned Rev Warner, who wrote in 1800 that "An idea of the immense population of the country in the environs of Manchester burst upon our minds on a sudden, when we reached the summit of a hill about two miles without the town, where a prodigious champaign of country was opened to us, watered by the river Irwell, filled with works of art: mansions, villages, manufactories, and that gigantic parent of the whole, the widely-spreading town of Manchester."(8) Compare this to the description of Manchester by the German writer V A Huber in 1844 - after nearly four decades of industrialisation: "Yes, it is a heavy, bleak, dreadful impression, this first view into the big, grey heart of industrial England... nowhere is the interest attracted to one outstanding or even pleasant... external feature. One must have to the highest degree the need, the instinct and the practice to find one point for the eye and the imagination and the memory amidst the vast uniformity of the streets and houses of Manchester... which have all been constructed purely to be functional... (London is) not only much greater, livelier, fresher and more colourful than Manchester, but it also has, through various transitions, something of the aristocratic dignity of the West End... all this is contrasted by Manchester... silent, ugly, serious, gloomy, almost threatening in its restless, gigantic but joyless activity... The more you try to read into the faces of these people here... the more you feel a hostility which is quiet, passive, more melancholic, dull and sad than passionately excited or exciting."(9)

A subject frequently remarked upon by visitors was Manchester's non-corporate status. Historically a market town administered almost as a feudal manor, Manchester had local government systems to match until 1838. The authority comprised the Lord of the Manor (most often a member of the Mosley family), the somewhat antiquated Court Leet and the Police Commissioners. More importantly, Manchester had no guild restrictions. This peculiarity was perceived by the German travel writer P A Nemnich, who, in his description of

Victor Huber

Manchester in 1799, compared the town with Wigan: "As Wigan is a corporate town the inhabitants did not allow anyone other than its corporation members (guildsmen) to enjoy the advantages of this trade (cotton manufacture). This made many inhabitants of Lancashire, who wanted to have a career as a cotton worker, settle down in Manchester, where they could not only live free from any similar legal constraints but also find the most suitable position to have access to an expanded trade."(10) Most of the other larger Lancashire towns had corporate status and this often restricted the development of their trade. In Manchester these commercial shackles did not exist and thus the town's peculiarities of local government played their part in stimulating its development into a regional centre of commerce. This was to be of crucial importance in the late eighteenth century. From this time rapid expansion and industrialisation led to an increasing demand to incorporate the town's local government and to give it the legal powers to tackle the new and alarming problems with which it was faced. The corporate status was granted in 1838.

Generally speaking, visitors to Manchester before 1800 praised the town, whereas after this time criticism is much more prevalent. The critics spotlighted a multitude of social and environmental problems such as excessive smoke, poor or non-existent sanitation, bad housing and many social abuses. However, Manchester was sometimes praised throughout this period for its factories, its technologically advanced machinery and its overall energy. The written accounts of the town take many forms. There are books on social conditions; parliamentary commissioners' reports; British and foreign

The Collegiate Church, 1795

newspaper articles; pamphlets by various pressure groups who were anxious to bring attention to some particular abuse; health and sanitation reports; travel guides and novels. The well known parliamentary commissioners' reports make horrifying reading. They identified such problems as "vaste open cesse pools", "dead dogs and cats to be seen in various stages of decomposition", the dreadful effects of the cholera epidemics and relatively minor problems like pigsties and dunghills - to name only a few. However, it should be said that these reports clearly point out the constraints on the infant Manchester Borough Council of inadequate or non-existent legal powers. In the first half of the nineteenth century, for example, the very poor sanitation in the town urgently needed to be tackled. Professor Redford has explained that "The Borough Council was not yet strong enough to solve its sanitary problems so systematically and comprehensively. For more than another generation, sanitary reform had in most directions to proceed tentatively and experimentally, by 'trial and error' and 'rule of thumb'... The legal weakness hindered paving and sewering in all the townships of the municipal borough, and there can be no doubt that Engels and other critics were justified about the slow progress of the work."(11)

The reports about Manchester in general, and the parliamentary reports in particular, certainly made an impact. This was rather subjectively expressed by the Frenchman Eugene Buret, who described Manchester in 1840, asserting that since the publication of these reports "people in general have not ceased worrying about the physical conditions of the poor in England."(12)

Newspaper articles about Manchester either referred to specific incidents or developments in the town or they discussed national or regional issues, mentioning Manchester merely as part of a more general theme. Good examples of the latter type are the reports by the accomplished and versatile Rhineland journalist Gustav von Mevissen.(13)

The gloomy portrayal of Manchester in nineteenth century novels has often been dismissed as deliberate bias or exaggeration in order to sell books. Indeed, the Manchester novelist Elizabeth Gaskell frequently incurred the wrath of the town's factory owners, who considered her portrayal of working class life unjustifiably harsh. However, Charles Dickens, who visited Manchester on several occasions, was certainly in no doubt as to his feelings towards the town: "So far as seeing goes, I have seen enough for my purpose, and what I have seen has disgusted and astonished me beyond all measure. I mean to strike the heaviest blow in my power for these unfortunate creatures."(14) The blow was heavy indeed. The nineteenth century novelists, and Dickens in particular, have contributed more than any other type of writer or propagandist to the popular image of a nineteenth century England full of bleakness and degradation.

Another dominant theme in visitors' descriptions is the contrast between eighteenth century and nineteenth century Manchester, both in appearance and in the conditions prevailing. The nature of the reality behind these contrasts has been a highly contentious argument among historians. This is obviously no place to discuss the merits of the opposing views in detail, but one point at least should be made. Many historians have an unfortunate tendency to confine their attention to the narrow view of wage earning and to assume that where a person earned x amount more money in the nineteenth century factory than did his or her eighteenth century rural counterpart, the former must have had a higher standard of living. Sterile arguments of this kind ignore the results of the industrial towns in human terms. Rural, pre-nineteenth century workers doubtless experienced harsh conditions and were subject to many abuses and deprivations, but in the large industrial towns these conditions were multiplied, and thus magnified to an alarming degree. The effects of poor sanitation and bad housing in a village might be minimal; in the new industrial towns, where congested streets were packed together with few open spaces, the dangers assumed horrifying proportions. It was only with the rise and expansion of these crowded and filthy towns that a breeding ground was provided for the appalling cholera epidemics. There were also the dangers presented by excessive smoke and by the new factory machinery which often exposed over-worked, under-supervised and inexperienced operatives to serious injury. Even if factory workers in the early nineteenth century were financially better off, the quality of their lives - and particularly their health and environment - simply must have been worse than in the pre-nineteenth century years.

Mrs Gaskell

Gustav von Mevissen

The overwhelming majority of written accounts by contemporary observers of Manchester and the other industrial towns express shock and disgust. It was not only the politically-motivated commentators like Engels and Marx who were horrified. There was, for instance, General Sir Charles Napier, who in 1839 was commanding the armed forces in the north of England, on stand-by to suppress the potentially violent Chartists. Napier wrote in his diary: "Manchester is the chimney of the world. Rich rascals, poor rogues, drunken ragamuffins and prostitutes form the moral; soot made into paste by rain, the physique; and the only view is a long chimney; what a place! The entrance to Hell realised."(15) Napier even felt a sense of regret in carrying out his orders: "Good God what work! To send grapeshot from four guns into a helpless mass of fellow citizens; sweeping the streets with fire and charging with cavalry, destroying poor people whose only crime is that they have been ill-governed, and reduced to such straits that they seek redress by arms, ignorant that of all ways that is the most certain to increase the evils they complain of." As early as 1808, the poet Robert Southey, in his bitter condemnation of Manchester's manufacturing system, declared: "What a happy country is England! A happy country indeed it is for the higher orders... In no other country can such riches be acquired by commerce, but it is the one who grows rich by the labour of the hundred."(16) A more familiar expression of this emotive form of criticism is the often-quoted passage, "I am not surprised to find you expressing your disgust at Manchester. It is a damned dirty den of muckworms. I would rather be hanged in London than die a natural death in Manchester. The Chartists there are the worst lot in the country."(17)

Another aspect of the new industrial towns in general, and of Manchester in particular, in which commentators and observers became increasingly interested was the sharp division of society into classes. Manchester exemplified this phenomenon and thus through the long residence of Engels in the town, the theory of class and class struggle became of fundamental importance to the philosophy of Marxism. Even writers such as the Irishman William Cooke Taylor, who was firmly committed to the capitalist doctrine, could not escape the conclusion that "The isolation of classes in England has gone far to divide us into nations as distinct as the Normans and the Saxons; in our wisdom we have improved on the proverb, 'One half of the world does not know how the other half lives', changing it into 'One half of the world does not care how the other half lives'. Ardwick knows less about Ancoats than it does about China, and feels more interested in the condition of New Zealand than of Little Ireland."(18)

A less obvious function of visitors to Manchester was that of industrial espionage. These clandestine enquirers, many of whom remain unidentified, were seldom concerned with writing descriptions of the appearance of the town, but they readily engaged themselves in studying the new industrial technology and organisation. Sometimes these spies were foreign manufacturers anxious to improve the efficiency of their machinery; on other occasions, foreign governments sent agents to the English industrial towns to compile reports for their ministries of trade. One industrial spy who combined both of these roles was Ernst Knapp (1834-1882) of Reutlingen in southern Germany. Knapp was a member of a prominent and locally-influential family of manufacturers and he was sent by the Prussian ministry of trade in Berlin to examine and report on the new manufacturing techniques in Manchester. He stayed for eighteen months at Tutbury Street in Ancoats and compiled an extensive file – complete with detailed and skilfully executed drawings – on Manchester's textile machinery.(19) These reports, and many others like them, helped to bridge the technological gap between British industrialists and their slower continental counterparts.

There were other visitors who were bent on researching a particular aspect of industry. One example among many is that of the German mineralogist Johann Ferbers, who visited Manchester in 1792. His only observation on the town was that "Splendid dye-works, cotton and cloth mills and shoe-lace factories are to be seen here."(20) The main obsession of Ferbers was the use of green vitriol in various chemical processes in the town's factories.

Among the least helpful descriptions of Manchester are those contained in the many town guides, maps, drawings and trade directories of the town. Most of these merely give a very basic account which is seldom based on first hand observation, and the same applies to road books, which were, in effect, forerunners of modern road atlases but usually included short descriptions of towns and points of interest along the various routes. A good example of the latter kind of work is John Ogilby's "Survey of the Roads of England" (London 1698), where a very 'standard' description of Manchester is appended to his maps and commentary on the region's roads.(21)

The authenticity of visitors' descriptions is sometimes questionable and there are frequent indications that more is owed to secondary sources and a fertile imagination than to first hand observation. Even when texts are not obviously derivative, they rarely offer reasonable evidence that the writers actually set foot in the town and we are thus often compelled to accept the word of the visitor that his account is trustworthy.

Just as visitors came to Manchester for a variety of reasons, so the style and content of their writings often reflected what they wanted to get from the town. Perhaps some also came with preconceived views, found only what they wanted to find and wrote their descriptions accordingly. For instance, a visitor sympathetic to the factory system and the new technological advances of the age would concentrate on these things and pay less heed to the more negative and darker aspects. Conversely, the critics focused on the social and environmental evils of this new society. In 1840 the American traveller C E Lester wrote, "These burdens (of the English working class) I have no desire to exaggerate. Would to God I could believe they have ever been exaggerated. For it would then be other than with a feeling of sadness that I have taken up my pen to write out the woes of some millions of the poor people of our Fatherland."(22) However, the charge of exaggeration must have at least some validity. One only has to consider how holidaymakers in our own time embroider their travellers' tales, whether it be in horror stories of half-built hotels or in rhapsodies on the idyllic fulfilment of their dreams. With all visitors' descriptions the only safe approach is to assess each case on its merits. This is especially true with Manchester, a town which, at least in the first half of the nineteenth century, tended to inspire the extremes of human feeling. At this time Manchester was the new and alarming

Sir Charles James Napier

phenomenon of the age; the symbol of the brave new world which embodied the creation of a new social and political order. It thus attracted countless visitors. It became the new fashion to see the shocks and wonders of Manchester, as visitors in previous ages had flocked to France and Italy to savour the great artistic creations. After the mid-nineteenth century the impact of Manchester became less because industrial towns like it became the rule rather than the exception.(23)

What will occupy the minds of visitors to Manchester in the future? Perhaps they will admire the transport facilities, the university, the shops, the museums or the surviving Victorian architecture. It is sobering to speculate on how many of them - or how few - will be attracted by Manchester's manufacturing industry as visitors were in the nineteenth century. Will they file through museums to witness what the city was, rather than what it is? How many would agree with the statement that "Manchester has become an agreeable provincial town but it is no longer one of the great cities"?(24) In a sense, Richard Cobden foresaw the fate of Victorian Manchester when, after visiting the ruins of a former civilisation at Pompeii, he wrote a letter from Rome to his old friend Sir John Potter over in Manchester. In the letter, dated 27th March 1827, Cobden asked, "Will tourists from New Holland or Michigan be someday amusing himself with digging up antique steam engines at Manchester?"(25)

Notes
1) Both von Popplau and the squire are quoted in W D Robson-Scott, "German Travellers in England, 1400-1800" (Oxford 1953), pp15 and 17 respectively.
2) J W Archenholz, "England und Italien" (2 vols, Leipzig 1785), I, 9.
3) F Engels, "Landscapes" in "Karl Marx/Frederick Engels Collected Works" (London/Moscow 1975), II, 99. Translated from the German by C Dutt.
4) W D Lenssen, "Reise nach England" in "Rheydter Jahrbuch für Geschichte, Kunst und Heimatkunde" (Mönchengladbach 1979), XIII, 56.
5) Engels, loc cit.
6) N Hawthorne, "Works" (Boston 1894) VIII, 285.
7) Rev R Warner, "A Tour through the Northern Counties of England" (London 1802), II, 144-145.
8) Warner, ibid, p140.
9) V A Huber, "Genossenschaftliche Briefe aus... England", II "England" (1855) p84.
10) P A Nemnich, "Beschreibung einer im Sommer 1799 von Hamburg nach und durch England geschehenen Reise" (Tübingen 1800), pp270-171.
11) A Redford, "History of Local Government in Manchester" (Manchester 1940), II, 143-145. A good bibliographical introduction to books on social conditions generally is in W H Chaloner and R C Richardson, "Bibliography of British Economic and Social History" (Manchester University Press 1984).
12) E Buret, "De la misere des classes laborieuses en Angleterre" (2 vols 1842), II, 215.
13) These reports are reproduced in J Hansen, "Gustav von Mevissen, ein rheinisches Lebensbild" (2 vols, Berlin 1906), II, 83-87 (photocopies are in the Manchester Local History Library). See also the "Rheinische Zeitung", 13/9/1842 and 18/9/1842 under the title "Englische Zustände" (microfilm, Manchester Local History Lib.)
14) Letter by Charles Dickens dated 29/12/1838 in "The Letters of Charles Dickens" ed M House and G Storey (Oxford 1965), I, 483. For the industrial towns in Victorian novels see K Flint, "The Victorian Novel and the Social Problem" (1986) and also vol VI of "The New Pelican Guide to English Literature" (1982) ed B Ford.
15) Napier's diary in W F P Napier, "The Life and Opinions of General Sir Charles Napier" (London 1857), II, 57 and, for the quotation following, 42.
16) R Southey, "Letters from England" (3 vols 1808), II, 87.
17) Letter by the Chartist leader Julian Harney in "The Harney Papers" (1969) ed F G and R M Black, p260.
18) W Cooke Taylor, "Notes of a Tour in the Manufacturing Districts of Lancashire" (1842; 1968 edn), p164.
19) The Ernst Knapp MSS, Staatsarchiv Ludwigsburg. For a discussion of German espionage in England, see K D Einbrodt and J Roesler, "Die Industriespionage Preußens in England in den Jahren 1790-1850. Eine Materialzusammenstellung" (Berlin 1962).
20) J J Ferbers, "Nachrichten und Beschreibungen einiger chemischen Fabriken..." (Halberstadt 1793), p106. For a list of eighteenth century German sources in general, see W D Robson-Scott, "German Travellers in England, 1400-1800", p205.
21) For a bibliography of road books, see H G Fordham, "The Road Books and Itineraries of Great Britain, 1750-1850" (Cambridge 1924).
22) C E Lester, "The Condition and Fate of England" (2 vols 1843), I, 93.
23) For a brilliant analysis of Manchester at this time, see A Briggs, "Victorian Cities" (1963), chapter 3.
24) A J P Taylor, "Essays in English History" (1950; 1976 edn), p307.
25) Manchester Central Library, Archives Department ref no M87/1/1/23.

From "An Illustrated Itinerary of the County of Lancaster", 1842

Above: Eight cardings combining into one

Above right: Calendering

Right: Calico printing

John Leland
(c1506-1552)

Although John Leland was born in London, he was probably descended from a Lancashire family. He was educated in London, Cambridge and Oxford and completed his historical and linguistic studies in Paris.

After taking Holy Orders, Leland attracted the attention of King Henry VIII, who granted him a small annual income, appointed him as his library keeper and invested him with the office of "King's Antiquary". Leland had neither predecessor nor successor in this office. The King commissioned Leland to travel all over England, to search through all libraries and to write descriptions of towns, villages and the countryside and record the peculiarities of local customs and legends.

Leland set out from London in 1535 and over the following eight years he amassed an astonishing collection of material, the result of which was a vivid, although rather disjointed, portrait of England's now obscure past.

Some time between 1535 and 1543 Leland found his way to the small Lancashire market town of Manchester and wrote the earliest known visitor's description of the town.

"Mancestre on the south side of Irwel river stondith in Salfordshiret,(1) and is the fairest, best buildid, quikkest and most populus tounne of al Lancastreshire; yet is in hit but one paroch chirch, but is a college and almost thoroughowt doble ilyd ex quadrato lapide durissimo, whereof a goodly quarre(2) is hard by the towne.

Ther be divers stone bridgis in the toune, but the best of iii arches is over Irwel, cawllid Salford bridge.(3) This bridge devidith Manchester from Salford, the wich is as a large suburbe to Manchester. On this bridge is a praty litle chapel.(4) The next is the bridge that is over Hirke river, on the wich the fair builded (college) standith as in the veri point of the mouth of hit. For hard therby it renneth into Wyver.(5) On Hirk river be divers fair milles that serve the toune.(6)

In the towne be ii fair market placys.(7)

And almost ii flyte shottes withowt the towne(8) beneth on the same side of Irwel yet be seene the dikes and fundations of Old Man Castel(9) yn a ground now inclosid.

The stones of the ruines of this castel wer translatid toward making of bridgges for the tounne.(10)

It is no long season sins the chirch of Manchestre was collegiatid.(11)

The toun of Manchestre stondith on a hard rokke of stone,(12) els Irwel, as wel apperith in the west ripe, had been noiful to the toune.

Irwel is not navigable but in sum places for vadys(13) and rokkes."

Further to this now very familiar account, Leland echoed an old local tradition that "Edward the Sunne of Alfred(14) repaired Manchester defaced by the Danes Warre." This continued to fuel the legend that Manchester had been laid waste by

John Leland

a Viking raid in pre-Norman times.

John Leland died in 1552, allegedly after a period of insanity induced by the labours of his long studies, and was buried at St Michael le Querne Church in London. This church was destroyed in the Great Fire and not rebuilt.

Notes
This text is taken from "The Itinerary of John Leland in or about the years 1535 to 1543" (1909), ed from the MSS by Lucy Toulmin-Smith, IV, 5-6.
1) "Salfordshiret" refers to the administrative area of the Salford Hundred.
2) These were the sandstone quarries at Collyhurst, the stone from which was used to build the Collegiate Church and the College.
3) This bridge dated from the fourteenth century and was demolished in 1839 and replaced by the present Victoria Bridge.
4) This chapel, located on the bridge itself, was first built in the mid-fourteenth century and rebuilt in 1505, when it was converted into a dungeon.
5) "Wyver" simply means the river - either the Irk or the Irwell.
6) These mills were situated on the banks of the Irk and included the Lord of the Manor's corn mill and also a fulling mill dating from at least the late thirteenth century.
7) These were the Old Market Place (now Shambles Square) and Acresfield. The latter was the site of an annual autumn market dating from 1223. The area is now indicated by St Ann's Square.
8) This means "at a distance of two arrow shots from the town".
9) This was the remains of the Roman fort at Castlefield which

Old Salford Bridge

was then amidst the woods of Aldport Park, the site of which is now the area between Quay Street and Knott Mill.

10) The only possible survivor of these bridges is the remains of the fourteenth century Hanging Bridge off Cateaton Street, near the south entrance of the Cathedral.

11) Manchester's parish church was designated as a collegiate foundation in 1421 and received cathedral status in 1847.

12) Here, Leland is alluding to the fact (difficult to appreciate today) that Manchester was built on a small but rocky cliff, and this protected it from floods.

13) "Vadys" means "fords". Leland states that the river was only partially navigable, because of the number of fords and rocks along its course.

14) This refers to King Edward the Elder, son of Alfred the Great, who ordered the rebuilding of Manchester c923.

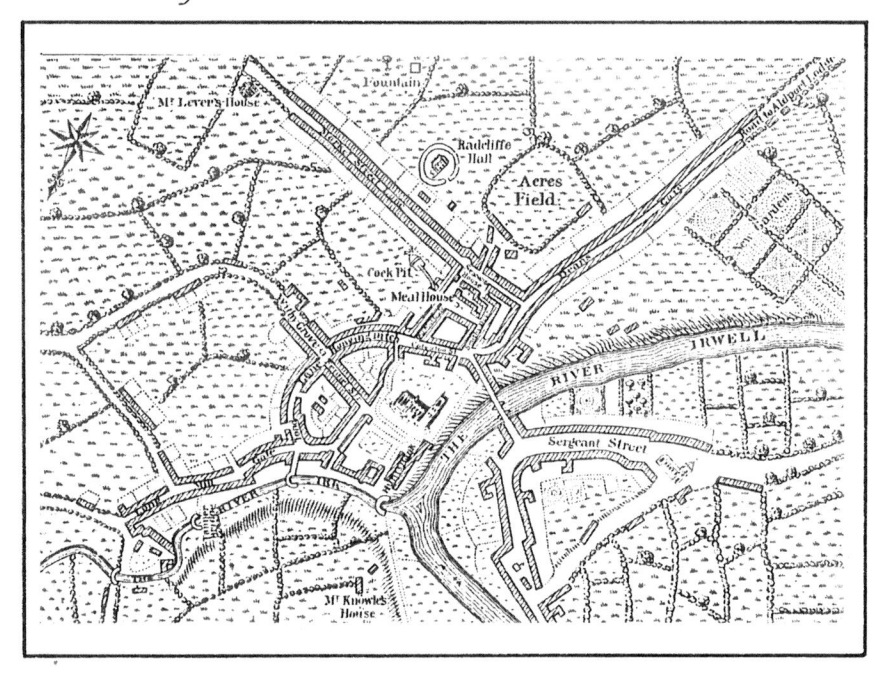

An impression of the Manchester & Salford plan, 1650

William Camden
(1551 - 1623)

The pioneering work of John Leland was developed with added skill and refinement by the great antiquaries in the age of Elizabeth I - especially by the next visitor known to have recorded his thoughts of Manchester, William Camden.

William Camden was born in London and, like Leland, had some family roots in Lancashire. After an education in London and Oxford, Camden became master of the prestigious Westminster School. His formidable researches, especially in the field of topography, culminated in his magnificent work "Britannia", which, soon after its publication, was translated into several European languages and became one of the standard reference sources for foreign travellers to England.

On November 9th 1623, Camden died after a painful illness of blood vomiting and paralysis. He was honoured with an interment in Westminster Abbey and his name is commemorated in the famous Camden Society.

There is one curious coincidence concerning William Camden. He was related to the Curwens of Workington in Cumberland, many of whom emigrated to New England in the seventeenth century. In 1777 Samuel Curwen, a descendant of these original emigrants, visited England and wrote a description of Manchester. Could it be that Samuel's ancestor was the famous William Camden?

In 1582 Camden arrived in Manchester and wrote:

"At the confluence of the Irwell and Irk, on the left bank, which is of reddish stone... stands that antient town called ...Manchester. This surpasses the neighbouring towns in elegance, populousness, a woollen manufacture, market, church, and college... In the last age it was much more famous for its manufacture of stuffs called Manchester Cottons,(1) and the privilege of sanctuary,(2) which the parliament under Henry VIII transferred to Chester. In a park of the Earl of Derby, in this neighbourhood, called Alpark, I saw the foundations of an old square tower, called Mancastle. ...(In) AD920, Edward the Elder... sent an army... to rebuild the town of Manchester and place a garrison there. For it seems to have been ruined in the Danish War; and the inhabitants say their town had its name from their brave stand against those invaders, Manchester signifying, according to them, the city of men, and they are wonderfully proud of an opinion so much to their honour. But these good people are not aware that Mancunium was its name in the British times, so that an etymology taken from our English language falls to ground. I should rather derive it from the British word Main, signifying a stone, it (the town) standing on a stony hill; and below the town at Collyhurst are noble and famous quarries."

Manchester's reputation as an expanding and wealthy market town must surely have been spreading throughout the sixteenth century. However, the traveller Fynes Moryson, who made a ten year tour of Europe in the early years of the seventeenth century, visited Manchester in 1617 and merely wrote that "Manchester is an old towne, fair and wel inhabited, rich in the trade of woollen cloth, is beautified by the market place, the church

William Camden

and the colledge and the clothes called Manchester Cottons are vulgarly known." (F Moryson, "Itinerary...etc" (London 1617), p144.)

Notes
The text is from "Camden's Britannia", ed R Gough, 2nd enlarged edn. (London 1806), III, 375-376.

1) The term "Manchester Cottons" actually refers to a type of coarse woollen cloth.
2) The privilege of sanctuary allowed certain categories of criminals legal impunity within the town. This privilege was removed to Chester, probably because it became less and less desirable to encourage criminals in the town as Manchester's wealth increased.

Celia Fiennis (1662 - 1741)

One of the very few women travellers who committed their impressions of Manchester to paper was the remarkable Celia Fiennis. She was born at Newton Toney, near Salisbury, and came from a strong non-conformist religious background. Celia Fiennis journeyed through England, mostly alone on horseback, in the closing years of the seventeenth century. In 1688 she descended from the windswept heights of Blackstone Edge to the town of Manchester.

"Manchester looks exceedingly well at the entrance, very substantiall buildings, the houses are not very lofty but mostly of brick and stone, the old houses are timber work, there is a very large church all stone and stands high soe that walking round the church yard you see the whole town; there is a good carving in wood in the Quire of the church ...Just by the church is the colledge... which is a pretty neate building with a large space for the boys to play in and a good garden walled in; there are 60 Blew Coate boys in it, I saw their appartments and was in the cellar and dranck of their beer which was very good... There is a large library 2 long walls full of books... and there I saw the skinn of a rattle snake 6 foote long... (and) the jaw of a sherk(1)... The market place is large it takes up two streetes length when the market is kept for their linen cloth cotten tickings incles,(2) which is the manufacture of the town; here is a very fine schoole for young Gentlewomen as good as any in London and musick and danceing, and things are very plenty here this is a thriving place."

The energetic work of Celia Fiennis has been favourably compared with that of another remarkable traveller of her generation, the celebrated Daniel Defoe (see page 11).

William Stukeley (1687 - 1765)

The physician and antiquary William Stukeley was born in the Lincolnshire village of Holbeach and was the son of an attorney. Stukeley studied medicine at Cambridge and it was there that he allegedly began to steal dogs in order to dissect and experiment upon them. He also continued his medical studies in London. One of Stukeley's contemporaries, the historian Thomas Hearne, said of him that he was "very fanciful" and a "mighty conceited man".

In 1725, Stukeley travelled through the wilds of northern England gathering material for his formidable book "Itinerarium Curiosum". Included in this work are some interesting observations on the increasingly prosperous town of Manchester.

"(Manchester is) the largest, most rich, populous and busy village in England. There are two thousand four hundred families. The site of the Roman castrum is now called Knock Castle.(1) They have a fabulous report of Tarquin a giant living there, killed by Sir Lancelot de Lake, a knight of King Arthurs(2)... A Roman altar (was) dug up here (at the Roman Fort)... and a large gold Roman ring... The Castle Field (has) the foundation of the wall and ditch remaining.

Some call it Man-castle: its name comes from the British maen, lapis, meaning its rocky soil. The old church, though very large, having three rows of neat pillars, was not capable of containing the people at divine service; whence they raised, by voluntary subscriptions, a new edifice after the London models, finished last year... Their trade, which is incredibly large, consists much in fustians, girth web, tickings, tapes, etc, which is dispersed all over the Kingdom, and to foreign parts: they have looms that work twenty four laces at a time, which was stolen from the Dutch.(3) The College has a good library for public use... There is a Free School maintained by a mill upon the river(4)... On the same river, for the space of three miles upwards, there are no less than sixty water mills. The town stands chiefly on a rock... About a mile off, at the seat of Sir John Bland,(5) is a Roman altar, lately dug up thereabouts: in the mosses, as they call them in this country, they often find reliques of antiquity, such as arrow heads, celts, pick-axes, kettles, etc, of brass; many are in the repository of the library... French wheat grows commonly hereabouts, much used among the poor people... they have likewise wheat with long beards like barley... and a great plenty of potatoes."

Stukeley's description of Manchester is complemented in an interesting way by a Portuguese traveller, Don Manuel Gonzales, a merchant of Lisbon who visited Manchester in May 1730. Gonzales' account of Manchester

Notes
The text is from C Fiennis, "Through England on a side saddle in the time of William and Mary" (1888 edn), pp186-187.
1) The snake skin and the shark's jaw were frequent objects of attention at the college, but they were given to Peel Park Museum in Salford.
2) The word "incles" refers to a type of linen tape.

William Stukeley

is so similar to Stukeley's that this could well be a case of plagiarism. However, Gonzales did have a few original comments to make. He observed that "In the marshy part of this county the natives burn turfs, which they have in great plenty... especially in Manchester and its neighbourhood. ...Manchester... is so much improved in this and the last century above its neighbours, that though it is not a corporation, nor sends members to parliament, yet, as an inland town, it has perhaps the best trade of any in these northern parts, and surpasses all the towns hereabouts in buildings and numbers of people, manufactures, and its spacious market place and college... Here is an ancient, though firm stone bridge over the Irwell, which is built exceeding high, because as the river comes from the mountainous part of the country, it rises of three miles above the town." (Gonzales' travel journal reproduced in J Pinkerton, "A General Collection of the best and most interesting Voyages and Travel in all parts of the World" (London 1808), II, 19 and 40.

Notes
The text is from "Itinerarium Curiosum" (London 1776), p58.
1) Supplementary to Stukeley's comments on the Roman fort is the description by the antiquarian John Horsley, who observed that "The ramparts (of the fort) are still very conspicuous." (J Horsley, "Britannia Romana" (London 1732), p415.)
2) There is no evidence to support this purely local legend.
3) It is likely that this machine was stolen or copied from Dutch artisans.
4) The income from the mills on the Irk continued to fund the Grammar School well into the nineteenth century.

The first Manchester Grammar School, c1519

5) Sir John Bland was the husband of Lady Ann Bland (nee Mosley). They dwelt at the beautiful mansion of Hulme Hall which was situated on the banks of the river Irwell near to Knott Mill. The site of the house is now covered by a railway viaduct near to the bottom of Hulme Hall Road, off Chester Road.

Daniel Defoe
(1660 - 1731)

Daniel Defoe was born in London and was the son of a butcher. Throughout his vigorous and varied life as a soldier, a journalist and a spy, he pursued a passion for political writings as well as for his more famous literary work.

Between 1724 and 1726 Defoe embarked upon a tour of Britain, observing through keenly astute eyes aspects of social and economic history which he described in passages ranging from the analytical to the anecdotal. After approaching Manchester from the flat wastelands of Chat Moss, Defoe penned his now well-known account of the town.

"(Manchester is) one of the greatest, if not really the greatest mere village in England. It is neither a walled town, city or corporation; they send no members to parliament; and the highest magistrate they have is a constable or headborough;(1) and yet it has a collegiate church, several parishes, takes up a large space of ground, and, including the suburb or the part of the town called Salford over the bridge; it is said to contain above fifty thousand people.(2)

The Manchester trade we all know... (it has) very much increased within these thirty or forty years... and as the manufacture is increased, the people must be increased of course. It is true, that the increase of manufacture may be by its extending itself farther in the country, and so more hands may be employed in the county without any increase in the town... But the increase of buildings at Manchester within these few years, is a confirmation of the increase of people; for that within very few years past... the town is extended in a surprising manner; abundance, not of new houses only, but of new streets of houses, are added, a new church also, and they talk of another, and a

The Chetham Library, 1797

fine new square is at this time building; so that the town is almost double to what it was a few years ago...

The town of Manchester boasts of four extraordinary foundations, viz. a college, an hospital, a free school,(3) and a library, all very well supported...

As for the antiquity of the place, the antiquity of the manufacture indeed is what is of most consideration; and this, though we cannot trace it by history, yet we have reason to believe it began something earlier than the great woollen manufactures in other parts of England...

I cannot doubt but this increasing town will, sometime or other, obtain some better face of government, and be incorporated, as it deserves to be."

Notes

The text is from D Defoe, "A Tour through the whole Island of Great Britain" (1726; Penguin edn 1971), pp544-546.

1) Defoe was not the first visitor, and certainly not the last, to comment upon the deficiencies of Manchester's local government. In 1704, the Bishop of Carlisle stayed in Manchester and wrote, "The Town is no Corporation or Burrough; but the largest ville in the Queen's Dominions." (C W Sutton, "Bishop William Nicholson's visit to Manchester", TLCAS vol XXII (1904), 187.)

2) This figure is almost certainly wrong. It has been alleged that Defoe deliberately overestimated the population of Manchester in order to further the cause for the town to be represented in parliament.

3) The "Free School" was Manchester Grammar School, which had been founded at Long Millgate in 1515 by Hugh Oldham, Bishop of Exeter. The school is now at Old Hall Lane in Rusholme.

Daniel Defoe

James Ray

(fl 1745)

In November 1745 Prince Charles Edward Stuart, the "Young Pretender" was entangled in his doomed quest to regain the English throne. However, his ill-equipped army only reached Derby before they retreated in the face of the disciplined soldiers under the command of the notorious Duke of Cumberland. Stuart's retreating force passed through Manchester, only to be pursued by his opponents. Amongst this latter contingent was a volunteer, James Ray, a native of Whitehaven, who later wrote an excellent account of the Jacobite Rebellion.(1) This book contains some interesting observations about Manchester.

"Manchester... may be stiled the greatest mere village in England... As this town is very populous, so the inhabitants are very industrious, driving an extraordinary trade in Fustian Manufactures, and that called Manchester Cottons for Women's wear, which it has been famous for for above 100 years, has been very much improved of late, by some inventions of dying and printing, which with great variety of other manufactures, known by the name of Manchester goods... enrich the town and render the people industrious, resembling those of Holland, the children here being all employed and earn their bread: They export vast quantities of their goods abroad, as to the West Indies. As an inland town, it has the best trade of any in these north parts... The buildings are the most sumptuous of any hereabouts. Here is a fine Gothic church, which is Collegiate... a very large, beautiful and stately Edifice, with a Choir (stall) remarkable for its neat and curious carved work..

St Ann's Square, 1746, from Berry & Casson's plan

Title page of James Ray's book

PLAN OF MANCHESTER & SALFORD 1751.

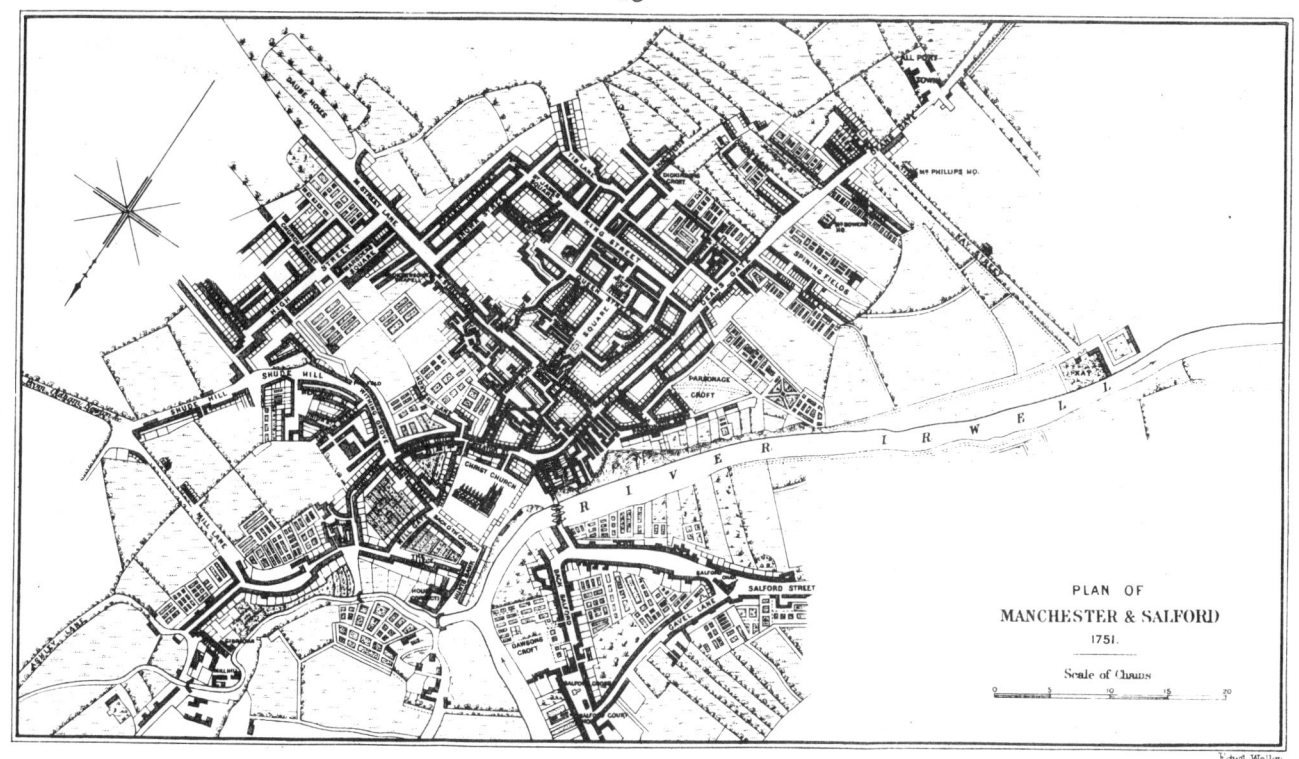

Here is an Hospital, a school, and a large library... where sixty poor boys are well maintain'd, cloathed and instructed in necessary learning and then put out Apprentices... (Because of the newly built St Ann's Church)(2) the town is very much improved by the building of a very handsome street of stately Houses, at the end of which the said church is erected. Near this church stands the Presbyterian Meeting House, which was pulled down by the Jacobite Mob at the time of the Rebellion in the Year 1715,(3) but was quickly re-built, and is now a very stately structure, not inferior to any in London. This town has a good market place and a modern Exchange, with many other eligant and magnificent buildings...

In this county the women are generally very handsome, by which they have acquired the name of Lancashire Witches, which Appellation they really deserve, being very agreeable."

Notes

The text is from J Ray, "A Compleat History of the Rebellion from its rise in 1745 to its total suppression" (York 1746), pp198-202.

1) Among the soldiers of the Stuart army was an Edinburgh man, the Chevalier de Johnstone, who also wrote a good account of the Rebellion. However, he merely said about Manchester that it was "a very considerable town of England, containing forty thousand inhabitants." (The Chevalier de Johnstone, "Memoirs of the Rebellion in 1745 and 1746" (3rd edn London 1822), p61.)

2) St Ann's Church had been built by Ann Bland, Lady of the Manor, as a platform for pro-Hanoverian preaching in opposition to the Collegiate Church, which was under Jacobite influence.

3) The ringleader of this mob, Thomas Syddall, was executed for this act of destruction.

Samuel Curwen
(1716 - 1802)

Samuel Curwen was a native of Salem, New England, and was educated at Harvard. On the outbreak of the American War of Independence (1775-1783), Curwen sought refuge in England and wandered somewhat aimlessly around the country. In 1777 his footsteps led him to Manchester.

"The centre of this town of Manchester consists principally of old buildings; its streets narrow, irregularly built, with many capital houses interspersed. By act of Parliament old buildings are taken down to enlarge the streets. It has few good ones; King Street is the best built, is long and sufficiently

Outside the first Exchange

wide; most of its houses noble. Great additions of buildings and streets are daily making...

The disposition and manners of this people, as given by themselves, are inhospitable and boorish. I have seen nothing to contradict this assertion, though my slender acquaintance will not justify me in giving that character. In all manufacturing towns there is a jealousy and suspicion of strangers; an acquaintance with one manufacturer effectually debars one from connection with a second in the same business. It is with difficulty one is admitted to see their works, and in many cases it is impracticable, express prohibitions being given by the masters. The (religious) dissenters are some of the most wealthy merchants and manufacturers here, but mortally abhorred by the Jacobites. The dress of the people here savours not much of the London mode in general; the people are remarkable for coarseness of feature, and the language is unintelligible.

We stepped into St John's Church, a small but elegant edifice in Gothic style; over the altar is a fine stained glass window... This church was finished in 1769; its tower is crowned with battlements and high pinnacles... From hence we adjourned to Castlefield, to see the exercise of the militia, making as good appearance as the King's troops in discipline and dress. This field is an eminence of oval form, and here are supposed to be the remains of an old Roman encampment, the outside wall and cement yet to be seen."

John Street, showing the church and manufacturers' houses

Notes
The text is from S Curwen, "The Journal and Letters of Samuel Curwen" (1844), pp134-6.

Johann Georg Büsch
(1728 - 1800)

The publisher and travel writer Johann Georg Büsch came from the German port of Hamburg and was the son of a priest. After completing his theological and mathematical studies in Göttingen and Hamburg, he embarked upon his travels around Europe. After visiting Scandinavia and Holland, Büsch found his way to England in 1777, but he had no great love for the English people. He often found them cold and inhospitable and he frequently derided their conceited tradition of freedom.

In his tour of England Büsch was concerned mainly with observations on the new and expanding industry and on the inland waterway navigations. His description is briefly interspersed into a more general discussion of the manufacturing industry of England. He also wrote an account of the Bridgewater Canal which has little value as it is largely derived from Hogrewe.(1) In September 1777 Büsch travelled from Derby and over the densely-clouded hills of the Peak District to Manchester.

"As in Birmingham,(2) the first thing that strikes you about Manchester is the bustle; a drive rewarded by ample profit and proven by the continuing growth of the town. However, more decorous public parks can be seen in Manchester(3) and so I came to the conclusion that the inhabitants here are of a different spirit which makes them want to enjoy life a little more. I have not been in Manchester long enough and the difference which I really noticed in the behaviour of the people does not really entitle me to say definitely that people in Manchester are more cheerful than in Birmingham, where I would almost like to say that people are working too much."

Within the context of growth in a capitalist economy, Büsch compared Manchester with, as he saw it, the relative backwardness of Salford. "Manchester is separated from the old town of Salford by the river Irwell which, at this point, is still a narrow river. Never could two towns in such close proximity form a sharper contrast than these two. I was told that this old town plays only a small part or no part at all in the activities of Manchester. This leads me to the remark that certain secondary circumstances are more relevant than usually assumed where means of transport and obstacles to industry are concerned. Once the creative ingenuity of our time is activated, it wants to see everything arranged in its own way. Nothing must stop it from procuring all the conveniences and individual comforts needed. In an old, smoke-ridden town with narrow, crooked alleys and leaning buildings full of nooks and crannies, ingenuity is not as thriving as in other places. It rather settles as I saw it here in Manchester and not in such a place as Salford."

Notes
The text is from J G Büsch, "Bemerkungen auf einer Reise durch einen Theil der Vereinigten Niederlande und Englands" (Hamburg 1786), pp 199,203-204.
1) J L Hogrewe, "Beschreibung der in England seit 1759 angelegten und jetzt grösstentheils vollendeten schiffbaren Kanäle" (Hanover 1780), pp135-151.
2) On his visit to Birmingham, Büsch made an interesting comment on the new building developments which must surely have applied to Manchester as well. He asked a builder why he was constructing a church when nobody lived anywhere in its locality. The builder merely replied, "Because the town will soon be here."
3) This statement that Manchester had several public parks is misleading. At the time of Büsch's visit, the only public park was the Infirmary Gardens (now Piccadilly Gardens). This was only added to after the agitation of the Public Parks Movement which resulted in the opening of Queens Park and Philips Park in 1846.

Johann Ludwig Hogrewe
(1737-1814)

The German engineer, geographer and cartographer Johann Hogrewe was a native of Hanover and in 1759 he joined the Hanoverian Engineering Corps. Hogrewe achieved particular distinction for his cartographic work on the German-speaking countries which had been commissioned by King George III of England. However, his most notable and influential study was his survey of the English canals and river navigations which was published in 1780. His book became a standard authority in Germany for anyone seeking information on this subject. Hogrewe compiled a very detailed account of the Bridgewater Canal, complete with many excellent maps and drawings. The extracts of his text quoted here are concerned only with the basin(1) of the Bridgewater Canal at Castlefield, not with the canal as a whole.

"Not far from Knottmill Bridge, a canal cut through rock leads underneath Castlefield, and almost at the end of it there is a round shaft which opens out above into the open air. A crane was standing over it, which, when set in motion by a waterwheel, hauled up the coal in crates of 800 pounds from the boats which are guided under this shaft. The advantage was that the coal could now be transported to the town on a level road instead of having to be carried up a hill which used to be quite difficult and expensive. There is a floodgate at the beginning of the canal which enables it to be closed and drained. The water which drove the wheel is directed by a narrow underground outlet into the river Medlock and so that the outlet, as well as the underground canal which leads away from the well, can be cleared of silt, there are in the water containers small wells closed with flaps through which water gushes. Owing to its quick drainage, the desired effect is achieved.

A few years ago, a storehouse was built at the foot of the hill above the underground canal; the laden boats can enter this and be unloaded by means of a lifting jack attached to the roof. The above mentioned waterwheel and crane, which were worthwhile inventions of Mr Brindley, have since fallen into disuse and the wells have been covered up.

There is still a lime kiln situated on the bank of the canal. A small channel, which can be closed by a floodgate, leads to it. The limestone and the coal are hoisted up in crates by a machine positioned on a slope. The limestone is crushed and both the limestone and the coal are thrown from the top into the furnace of the kiln. This machine is set in motion by a horse, which is walking around at a pole and turning a vertical shaft with its cylinder so that the rope, which is attached to the crate and goes over two spools, winds itself around the cylinder and pulls up the load to the top. The floor of the crate consists of two boards with bolts. They are kept together by a chain, which has been pulled through underneath and hung up at the other end over a hook so that, when the chain is loosened, the load falls out by itself...

Before I leave this area, I must make a few passing comments about Manchester. It is one of the most populous towns in England, and it is especially famous for its considerable velvet, plush, silk and ribbon factories. The number of people employed in these trades in the town and in its vicinity is astonishingly high. Thirty thousand people are said to be working in the town and fifty thousand outside. ...The ribbon looms are so ingeniously constructed that one single person is able to produce twenty or more pieces on it all at once.

The new St John's Church, which is of medium size, deserves all the more to be commented upon, because it was built out of the best ashlar in the years 1768 and 1769 for and at the expense of a Mr Brown.(2) The church is also distinctive in that it is built

Hogrewe's plan of the Bridgewater Canal

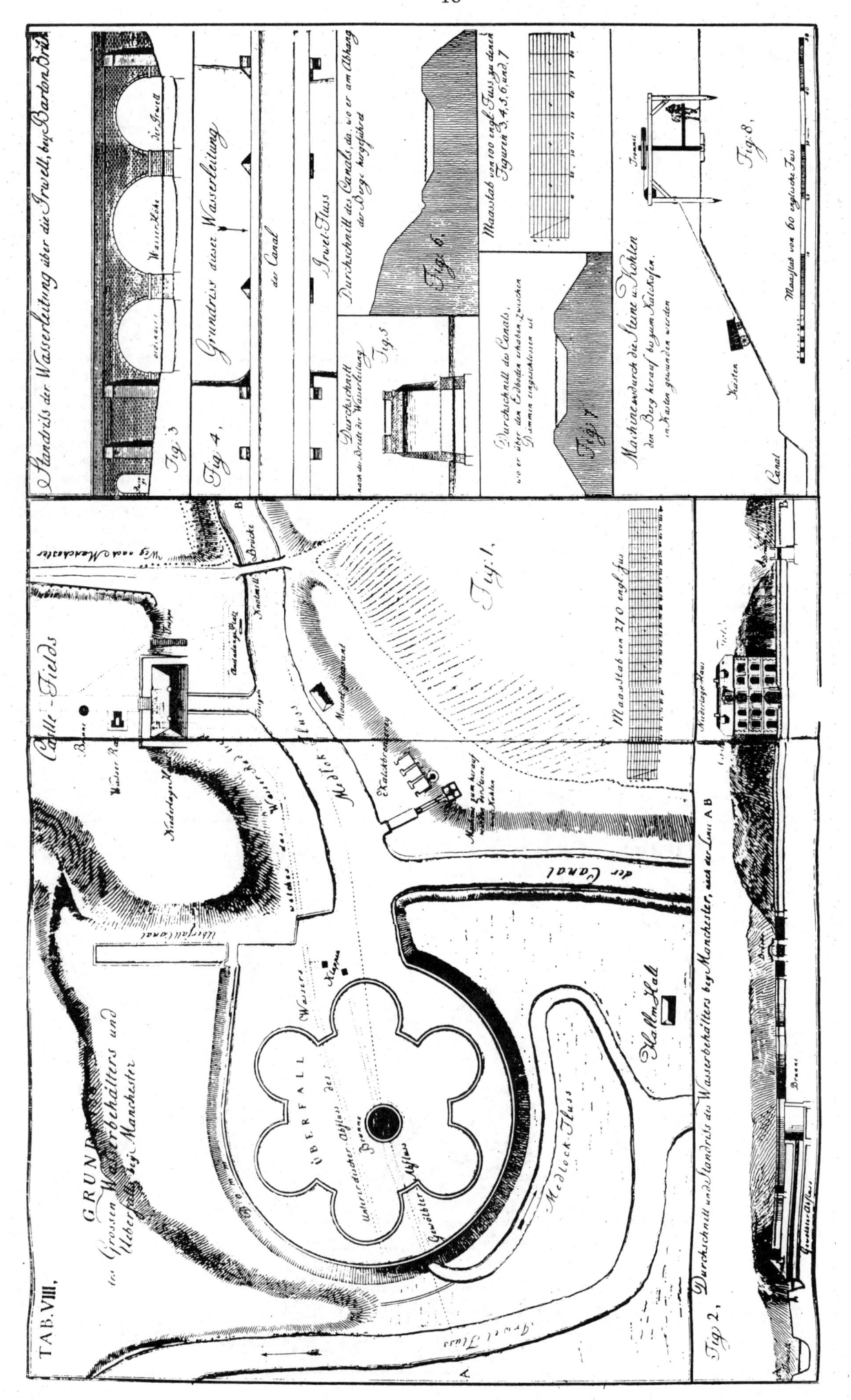

Hogrewe's plan of the Castlefield basin and cross-sections of the Bridgewater Canal (on the outside) completely in the old Gothic style, but the interior is furnished in a most excellent manner. The stained glass windows, which can compete with the most famous ones, prove that the art of painting on glass is not yet lost. The houses of the clergymen are near at hand and the outsides of the buildings are decorated in Gothic style in order to keep them in harmony with the church."

Notes

The text is from J L Hogrewe, "Beschreibungen der in England seit 1759 angelegten und jetzt gröstentheils vollendeten schiffbaren Kanäle..." (Hanover 1780) pp 145-147. Hogrewe's name also has the spelling of Hogrefe.

1) In 1771 the agricultural writer Arthur Young visited Manchester and viewed the Castlefield basin. He declared that "The general design of these works is, undoubtedly, great; the whole plan shows a capacity and extent of mind which foresees difficulties, and invents a remedy before the evil exists... I venerate, no less than the warmest of his (Brindley's) admirers, the masterly genius that planned them." Young also added the curious complaint, "It is a strange affair, that the town of Manchester does not possess a boat for the accommodation of its own inhabitants, and strangers who come to see it; for want of one, you may very probably wait a day or two." (A Young, "A Six Months Tour through the North of England" (London 1771), III, 199, 213.)

2) This name should be Edward Byrom. He had the church at Quay Street built to commemorate his father, the celebrated John Byrom. The church was consecrated in 1769 and was demolished in 1931.

St John's Church, 1816 (from Aston's "Picture of Manchester")

Johann Jakob Volkmann
(1732 - 1803)

Johann Volkmann was born in Hamburg and was the son of a wealthy lawyer. After an education in Leipzig and Göttingen, Volkmann spent one and a half years in Italy and nearly two years in France and he also extensively toured Spain and the Low Countries.

Between 1780 and 1782 Volkmann wrote a detailed, four-volume account of what seems to be a wide-ranging journey around England. However, there are serious doubts as to the authenticity of his book and particularly of his lengthy description of Manchester. In 1826 fellow German travel writer Johann Heinrich Meidinger stated that Volkmann's book was "difficult to assess because the author himself was never in England" and that the many unreliabilities in his descriptions largely stemmed from his use of English secondary sources such as "Tour through the Islands of Great Britain" (4 vols, London 1778)(1). On the other hand, a usually very reliable source records that in 1761 Volkmann, in the company of his brother Peter, toured Holland and England.(2) Furthermore, Volkmann's books were published in 1788 in a collection of the best travel descriptions of the period.(3) Nevertheless, there are clear indications in Volkmann's description of Manchester that he at least leaned very heavily on earlier published accounts of the town. For instance, his description of the remains of the Roman fort at Castlefield is, as is suggested in his acknowledgement in a footnote, probably derived from Whitaker.(4) Volkmann admits that his account of the Bridgewater Canal (not included in the extracts which follow) is taken from the writings of Hogrewe and Young(5). He also extracted - almost word for word - the description of St John's Church from the writings of Hogrewe and the section where Volkmann discusses the fame of Manchester's textile industry is too similar to von Tauber's account of the town for comfort.(6) More significant is the fact that Volkmann plagiarised the description of Manchester's textile trade from Arthur Young.(7) Perhaps Volkmann paid only a fleeting visit to Manchester - presuming he came to England at all - and later compiled his description from secondary sources. In Volkmann's defence it can be said that it is hard to believe that all four of his large volumes on England were compiled solely from books and that he deliberately deceived both publisher and public. Nevertheless, the derivative nature of his work shows how cautious a modern reader needs to be in assessing travel reports.

"Manchester is a large and wealthy town, more populous and more neatly built than most others in England. Nevertheless, in terms of the English Constitution it is not actually a corporate town, but it is only governed by a Constable and a Deputy Constable. One says, therefore, that Manchester is the largest market town in the Kingdom whose inhabitants do not have the right to send a member to represent them in Parliament. The town consists of... many large and small streets, an attractive market place, an exchange building(8) and a pleasant town square... (Old Salford Bridge is) an old and very substantial stone bridge... which was built to a considerable height because... water from the hills can raise the level of the river from four to five yards in twenty-four hours...

About one mile from the town one can still see the Roman fort; it is called Castlefield. There is a wall all the way round which is more or less still standing, but the ditches are in a more ruinous condition. The enclosed area of the fort consists of four to five acres and is called Mancastle. The fort has the natural defence of the river Medlock. Many Roman coins and inscribed objects have been found here...

Some of the new streets are so splendid that they are in no way inferior to the best in London. Of the public buildings, the Exchange, which is adorned with Greek columns, is especially noteworthy. The Collegiate, or St Mary's Church, is a large, beautiful, well-funded building dating from the fifteenth century. In the choir stalls there are some very artistic wood-carvings. St Ann's Church is a new and tastefully designed edifice which had been constructed on the authority of the town's richest inhabitant. Together with its tower, it gives St Ann's Square its good appearance. (St John's Church) is of medium size and built in the old Gothic style... with a splendidly furnished interior. The stained glass windows, which can compete with the most famous ones, prove that stained glass window making is not a lost art...

In the Free School, which educates forty poor boys, is a beautiful public library... Generally speaking, there are few towns in England where so much was given to the poor and where there are so many good institutions of all kinds than in this place.

The considerable trade of the town has made Manchester grow so quickly that one can compare it with York, Chester, Gloucester and even Norwich...

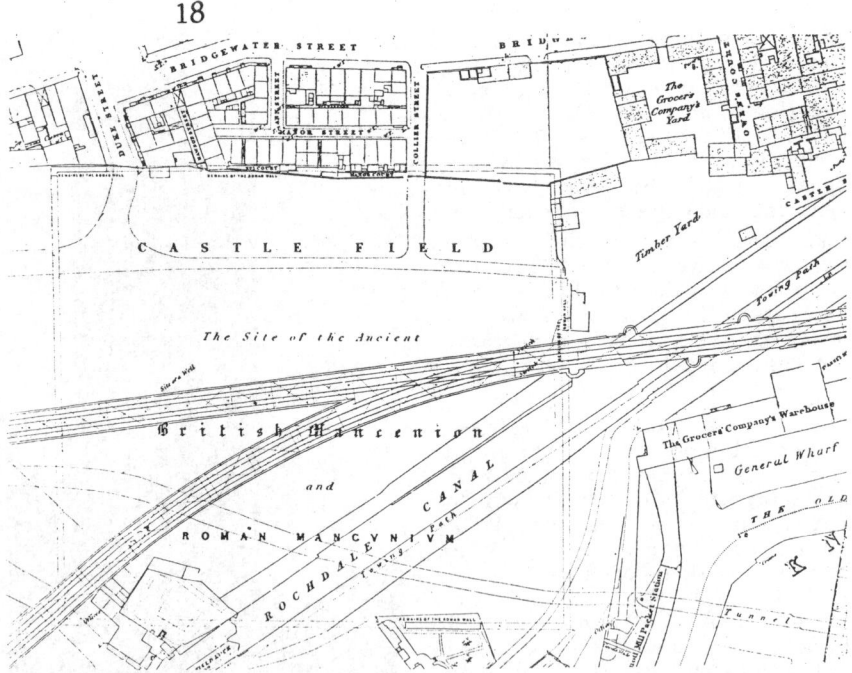

Plan showing site of Roman fort, based on 1849 Ordnance Survey

The quantity, beauty and multiplicity of the products which are made of wool, cotton, silk, flax and mohair are most admirable and it has enriched the whole of the surrounding area. The plain and floral-patterned plush and the so-called Manchester or Cotton velvet is known all over Europe...

All workers can, if they want, have continual work and this work continues in a very orderly manner, for the manufacturers do not wait for work before they employ people, but they rather keep their workers in wages and bread in the expectation of spring orders...

On the whole one notices with all of these very different classes that it is best for the workers when the prices of food are somewhat higher. The workers, as well as their women and children, are in such times better dressed, they eat and drink better and, generally speaking, are in better circumstances than when prices are low...

Numerous families here are no great burden because all hands are capable of earning something. It is said, therefore, that more money flows in this town in a single month than in the county of Huntingdon in half a year."

Further to these comments on Manchester's trade, Volkmann reproduced a list of wages paid to textile operatives in the town and also a breakdown of the many branches of the textile industry there. These, however, have no value as they are taken directly from the writings of Young, who, in turn, was given the information by the textile manufacturers Bell and Hamilton of St Ann's Square.

Notes

The text is from J J Volkmann, "Neueste Reise durch England, vorzüglich in Absicht auf die Kunstsammlungen, Naturgeschichte, Oekonomie, Manufakturen und Landsitze der GroBen" (4 vols, Leipzig 1781-1782), IV, 261-277.

1) J H Meidinger, "Reisen durch GroBbritannien und Irland, vorzüglich in topographischer, kommerzieller und statistischer Hinsicht" (Frankfurt am Main 1828), II, ii.
2) "Allgemeine Deutsche Biographie" (Leipzig 1896), XL, 237-238.
3) "Sammlung der besten Reisebeschreibungen" (1788), vol XXVIII.
4) J Whitaker, "History of Manchester" (London 1771).
5) Young, vol III; Hogrewe, pp135-151. Hogrewe's description of St John's Church is on p147.
6) About 1776, the Austrian traveller Friedrich Wilhelm von Tauber toured England and compiled a detailed study of its trade and manufacturing industry. However, von Tauber's description of Manchester's place in the world of commerce is surprisingly sketchy. He wrote that "Manchester, in the county of Lancaster, excels among the large towns of Europe in terms of its large population, its wealth, its splendid streets and its excellent buildings. It is the centre of all manufacture where wool, cotton, silk, flax and mohair are made. The quantity, beauty and multiplicity of these products is amazingly large and it has enriched the whole of the surrounding area which now swarms with manufacturers. ...The beautiful Manchester

velvet is known all over Europe. Although Manchester is not far from Norwich and although both towns are the main manufacturers of wool, silk, cotton and flax, there is a considerable difference between the products of these two towns. Both of them produce beautiful and excellent goods, but each has a wholly different mixture and type of work." (F W von Tauber, "Schilderung der Engländischen Manufakturen, Handlung, Schiffahrt und Colonien, nach ihrer jetztigen Einrichtung und Beschaffenheit" (Vienna 1777), part I, 116-117.
7) Young, III, 187-194.
8) This was the first Exchange which was built at the instigation of Sir Oswald Mosley at St Mary's Gate in 1729. It was demolished in 1792.

Grammar School, 1776

John Byng
(1740 - 1813)

The reminiscences of his tour through England and Wales by John Byng (5th Viscount Torrington and nephew of the famous Admiral Byng) reflect the writer's detached and critical viewpoint. Byng negotiated the horrific roads of north-west England in 1790 and, after passing through Salford, where he bewailed, "the noise and drunkenness of the artisans quite overcame me", he took rest at Manchester.

"At last I came to the great noisy hotel the Bridgewater Arms,(1) whose clamour, bell-ringing and want of attendance would drive a man wild.(2)

After breakfast I wandered

The first Exchange, built 1729. (from Berry & Casson's plan)

about this great, nasty manufacturing town... their Exchange is an hansome building, but crouded up in a low situation. Their market seems to be a bad one...

I tried various booksellers' shops and one brokering shop, for old books, but all in vain; then to the Collegiate Church, just at prayer time; where the singing was too bad to tempt my continuance: the old, massive stalls are very venerable, but their are no monuments, or stain'd glass about the church.

From the churchyard most of the old town is to be seen. Adjoining is the College... where, unask'd and uncontroll'd, I entered the old hall, walk'd the cloisters, and then ascended into the library... where the librarian was adjusting the books.

THE Public are most respectfully informed the
HIGHFLYER COACH,
to Leeds, York, Hull, &c. (carrying four insides only) will, on and after the 1st day of May, leave the Bridgewater Arms, High-street, every Morning at six o'clock, through Rochdale, Halifax, and Bradford, to the Rose and Crown Inn, Leeds.
Performed by
H. C. LACY and Co.
Coaches from the above Inn to London, Birmingham, Liverpool, Chester, Sheffield, and all parts of the west, also to Preston, Lancaster, Carlisle, Glasgow, Edinburgh, and all parts of the north, daily.

Advertisement for coaches from the Bridgewater Arms, High Street, 1822

I saw many soldiers about the town, and some officers in our coffee room... and I could scarcely credit the assertion of there being a regiment of Dragoon Guards...

(The new part of the town was) hourly increasing in buildings, and of the better sort; opposite to Lever's Row(3) is the grand new infirmary; and in Mosley Street, now finishing, are chapels for prayer and assembly rooms for dancing, well-built and bespeaking opulence and an increasing trade...

Who but a merchant could live in such a hole; where the slave, working and drinking a short life out, is eternally realing before you from fatigue or drunkenness."

Notes
The text is from "The Torrington Diaries", ed B Andrews (1935), II, 205-210.
1) The Bridgewater Arms was a coaching inn on High Street. The licence was later transferred to the Royal Hotel, Market Street.
2) Byng was not alone in his frustrations with Manchester inns. In 1788 the travelling musician Charles Dibdin indignantly complained that "At Manchester there is not a single good inn and the treatment is insolent beyond description." (C Dibdin, "Musical Tour" (1790), p279.)
3) Lever's Row was the name of the road on the north side of Piccadilly Gardens (the Oldham Street side).

Mosley Street Chapel

William Philips
(fl 1792)

On the Sunday morning of 13th May 1792, William Philips set forth from his home in the beautiful Cotswold village of Broadway in Worcestershire to journey on horseback to Lancashire. The following Saturday he ambled into Manchester from Ashton-under-Lyne. During his two-day stay in the town Philips penned a reasonably legible but rather garbled description of the main attractions of Manchester as he saw them.

"The first place we went to see was an old church, that has a great deal of antique carving in it with many very curious figures in wood. Then went and saw a large old school or college given and supported by one Cheatem,(1) upstairs we saw many rooms full of books piled up... to the ceilings and many serpents, lizards, monkeys etc with many stones and balls of hair that had been taken out of cattle when killed, with skeletons of several sizes and many curiosities of different sorts,(2) we then went down in the cellar and tasted the beer that the boys drink which was very good, saw some remarkable large loaves of bread and a large knife that's fixed to the bench to cut the bread for milk or broth which they have in wooden piggins... this place is kept very clean and neat. From here we went to the Old Quay(3) where the vessels load and unload upon the river Mersey. A very large quantity of goods of all kinds, timber, stone etc to be seen here... We then went to the Duke of Bridgewater's Quay and saw the

The Quay, 1742 (from Berry & Casson's plan)

vessels sail into the warehouses and a great quantity of corn in there of all sorts, tradesmen's goods etc... Then we went to see the New Bailey Prison,(4) this is a new built place and very grand it is, too good for some that are brought there, it is more like a nobleman's house and gardens walled round on the outside to appearance than a prison. There are several cells with rooms in for those that are fustian weavers to work in and some for fustian cutters, there is 124 separate cells and kept very clean and neat... (Next) we went to see the baths at the infirmary.(5) Here is a hot and cold bath for the ladies and a hot and cold bath for the gentlemen, with private dressing rooms for both, kept very clean and neat The Infirmary is a very large, handsome building with pleasant gardens to walk in and a large water with iron palisades before the front."

Notes

The text is from the journey of William Philips, taken from the original MS in the British Library (ref no ADD 30173).

1) The "one Cheatem" here referred to is Humphrey Chetham (1580-1653), a prominent and very wealthy Manchester woollen merchant, whose will provided the funds for the foundations of the famous Chetham's Library and poor boys' school (now a renowned music college) at Long Millgate.

2) These strange objects, like the aforementioned snake skin and shark jaw, are no longer in the possession of the library.

3) This is a reference to the quay on the river Irwell (near to the present Granada Television studios), where cargoes were unloaded after a journey from Liverpool along the rivers Mersey and Irwell. The enterprise was owned by the Mersey and Irwell Navigation Company, which had been established in 1720; it was taken over by the Bridgewater Canal Company in 1779.

4) New Bailey Prison was opened in April 1790, largely at the instigation of John Howard, a well known prison reformer, and it was often considered superior by contemporary standards. In August 1800 the German Ludwig von Vincke briefly visited Manchester and he singled out the prison as "exemplary" of its kind. (L von Vincke, "Briefe und amtliche Schriften", I, 497.)

5) The Infirmary and Lunatic Hospital were built at Piccadilly in 1775 on land owned by the Mosley family. The "large water" was the Infirmary Pond, now indicated by Piccadilly Gardens.

Philip Andreas Nemnich (1764 - 1822)

Philip Andreas Nemnich of Hamburg had two consuming passions, travel and writing. He completed exhaustive tours of Britain in 1799, 1805 and 1806 and his literary and journalistic output was considerable.

In 1799, as Nemnich was preparing for his first journey to England, he was requested to write reports of his travels for the Tübingen newspaper, the "Allgemeine Zeitung". However, the subsequent articles became so detailed that it was decided to publish them in book form. Nemnich's observations are intelligent, well-balanced and wide-ranging. His book also includes fascinating chapters on textile terminology and the dialects of the north of England.

Unlike many visitors to Manchester, Nemnich was not content merely to record the familiar objects of attention; he also made an attempt to explore the complex avenues of the town's economic history and the state of trade there at the time of his stay.

"This town is known throughout the world for the manufacture of cotton; but it is hardly more than a name to foreigners. Whatever has been written about it should not be taken too seriously, as it is rather likened to groping in the dark. What I now give can, in my opinion, make some claim to being complete. It is the work of many friends in Manchester who have so kindly taken the trouble to satisfy my desire for information on all subjects.

At the end of the last century Manchester was quite insignificant and could have had no more than a few thousand inhabitants; for in 1717 the number was only 8,000. In the year 1757 there were 19,839 and by 1773 29,151. From this time on the number increased considerably and despite the fact that many hands became redundant because of the introduction of machines, machinery itself produced new sorts of trade and the great expansion of the main trade of the town made (the demand) for more and more people necessary. The town expanded on all sides and the influx of inhabitants grew so much that a number of houses were lived in before they were even finished. The nine year American War in no way hindered the growth of trade here; for the merchants always found means of delivering their goods to their former markets...

Manchester is very irregularly built, as are almost all towns in England, where the inhabitants site their buildings and houses largely according to the convenience of their trade. In the older parts of the town there are many narrow streets

St Peter's Church, as it appeared in Aston's "Picture of Manchester", 1816

and a multitude of back-streets and cross passages,(1) so that a stranger even after a considerable amount of time can go astray. As can, of course, be expected of such a town, there are many large and beautiful houses. Of the various churches, St Peter's(2) is the most recent. It is built in similar style to (St Peter's) in Rome, but it is very small and still without a tower, because, it is said, the subscribers had not enough money. The common people may not visit this church which is only for the use of gentlemen. The Infirmary is a beautiful, very clean building, equipped according to the most excellent principles; nearby there are also baths and a lunatic hospital, the best part of which is called the Asylum. There is also a lying-in hospital for poor women. For amusement there is a theatre, concert halls, assembly rooms and so on.

The market place is not sufficiently large or imposing for a town such as Manchester. The centre of it is raised somewhat and is called the Exchange...

In Manchester continuously rainy weather prevails for most of the time; and when it will not stop raining in London they call it 'Manchester Weather'.

In the old college building, which has stood since 1422, there is a library which was founded by Humphrey Chetham; it contains good, and in some cases, rare books... As I went downstairs (in the college) I saw a swarm of orphans with their teacher, on their knees in prayer, in deepest silence. As soon as this mechanical act was finished with, there was a general cry and the boys dashed over the tables and pushed out through the door. What I could make out of the words uttered by these youngsters was mostly in the way of angry cursing. The boys who had been praying then went off to play and they seemed to get the greatest satisfaction in wrestling. Such lads will turn out to be fine fellows in later life...

The bookshops in Manchester are of no importance. There are a few circulating libraries. At the Bridgewater Arms, the leading inn at Manchester, there is a large room given over to a reading society...

In Manchester there are numerous meeting houses for all sorts of religious sects. One evening I attended a meeting of the Society of Shakers (Jumpers) of Wales.(3) The proceedings were carried on by a crowd of common people in a filthy room

A
DESCRIPTION
of
THE COUNTRY
from thirty to forty Miles round
MANCHESTER.

The Materials arranged, & the Work composed,

By J. AIKIN, M.D.

Embellished with seventy-three Plates.

LONDON.
Printed for John Stockdale, Piccadilly.
June 4. 1795.

Title page of Aikin's description

without a single unbroken window. They mostly made quite frightening grimaces and all kinds of peculiar movements in dancing and jumping and at the same time howled so pitifully that my eyes filled up with tears...

The first known trade of the inhabitants of Manchester was the production of leather laces and leather edges (borders) or lace (Congleton points). They wove a similar kind of lace or pinked ribbon for which they needed Dutch looms...

In 1763 the Velverets first appeared, followed a few years later by the Velveteens. These cloths became very popular all over Europe and have since been sold in such quantities that abroad they were mostly called "Manchester", especially the black cloth...

Towards 1763 the following houses in Manchester started to do direct business with Germany: Edmund Radcliffe, Harrison, Haughton and Douglas. It is believed that Edmund Radcliffe did most to expand commerce widely, for his trade was the largest and he worked extensively to establish links with all ports of the world by sending them samples. This resulted in a boom for Manchester and encouraged new improvements in weaving, dyeing and finishing cotton fabrics."

While in Manchester Nemnich gave currency to the many

doubts cast on the inventiveness of Richard Arkwright, whose fame and wealth rested on his innovations with textile machinery. Nemnich stated that "Arkwright's machine had scarcely been in operation when he was accused of not having invented it himself but of having borrowed the idea from others. Although this is common rumour, it is still Arkwright's merit to have introduced and used the machine." However, Nemnich did admit that "The yarn produced by the machine was not only of better quality and cheaper, but it could also be used as warp."

Amongst the more unusual observations about Manchester are the comments made by Nemnich on the history books written about the town. He felt that the Rev John Whitaker's often criticised "History of Manchester" (1771) was "very learned and much more an ancient history of the whole of England, in the course of which Manchester is incidentally mentioned and for the most part conjecturally, than a history of Manchester." Nemnich was singularly unimpressed with Ogden's "A Description and History of Manchester" (1783), which he condemned as "very incomplete and contains many errors". He held a similarly low opinion of Aikin's "A Description of the Country from 30 to 40 miles around Manchester" (1795), which he considered was "far from being complete and interesting, (and) is really a book for the amateur of fine books to display."

On the subject of maps of Manchester, Nemnich dismissed Laurent's map of 1793 as inaccurate, saying that it was drawn "not as the town is actually built, but as, according to his better judgement, the town ought to have been built. Such a plan, to my mind, is of no value."

The Manchester Literary and Philosophical Society had been founded for the purpose of promoting literature and science. However, Nemnich became aware of certain deficiencies in the society, complaining, "I have searched all the volumes (of the society), expecting to find much in them about the state of trade in Manchester, about the improvements in manufacturing, new inventions etc. But I discovered nothing of the kind."

The description and analysis of Manchester by Nemnich is one the more important commentaries to have been made of the town. Few visitors to eighteenth century Manchester took the time and trouble to give the town a close inspection. Nemnich was one of the very few.

Notes
The text is from P A Nemnich, "Beschreibung einer im Sommer von Hamburg nach und durch England geschehenen Reise" (Tübingen 1800), pp266-331.
1) Nemnich is complemented on this point by the historian John Britton, who acquainted himself with Manchester around the year 1805 and declared that "Manchester is an immense manufacturing, mercantile and trading town, consisting of a great number of streets, lanes, alleys, and courts, which are crowdedly filled with warehouses, factories and shops. At the extremities of the town, however, ...are many comfortable and handsome houses." (J Britton, "The Beauties of England and Wales" (London 1807), II, 251.)

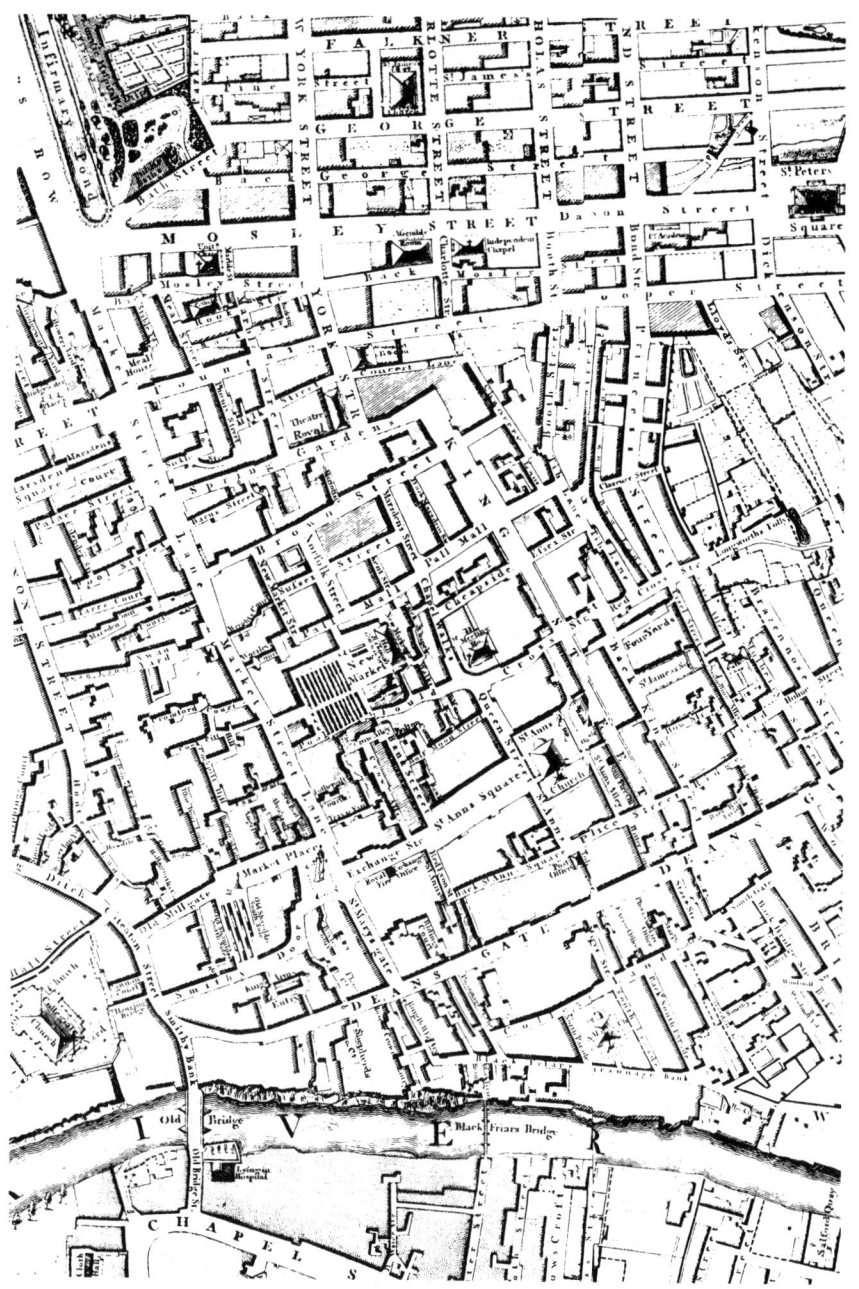

Part of Laurent's plan, 1793

2) St Peter's Church was built largely at the instigation of the friends of the Rev Samuel Hall, who became its first minister. According to the Manchester historian Joseph Aston, who witnessed the construction of the church, the delay with the steeple was due to a prolonged argument over whether it should be a steeple or a dome. The church was consecrated in 1794 and was demolished in 1906. Its site is now indicated by the Cenotaph in St Peter's Square.
3) The "Shakers" were a religious sect who had split from the Quakers in 1747. Their derogatory name was derived from their inclination to make involuntary movements in moments of religious ecstasy and in sacred dances. After the 1860s the sect began to decline.

Robert Southey
(1774 - 1843)

The celebrated poet and historian Robert Southey was educated in his native town of Bristol and also at Balliol College, Oxford. His prolific and varied work gained some prestige when he was appointed Poet Laureate, although admittedly this was only after the honour had been declined by Sir Walter Scott.

In 1808, Southey produced a lively account of England, written in the guise of a Spanish traveller, Don Manuel Alvarez Espriella (the pseudonym probably derived from the poet's passion for Spain and Spanish literature). During the course of his tour, Southey found his way to the town of Manchester.

"A place more destitute of all interesting objects than Manchester is not easy to conceive. In size and population it is the second city in the Kingdom, containing above four score thousand inhabitants. Imagine this multitude crowded together in narrow streets, the houses all built of brick and blackened with smoke; frequent buildings among them as large as convents, without their antiquity, without their beauty, without their holiness; where you hear from within, as you pass along, the everlasting din of machinery; and where, when the bell rings it is to call wretches to their work instead of their prayers... Imagine this, and you have the materials for a picture of Manchester.

The most remarkable thing which I have seen here is the skin of a snake, fourteen English feet in length, which was killed in the neighbourhood and is preserved in the library of the Collegiate Church. We left it (the Town) willingly on Monday morning...

(A guide) took us to one of the great cotton manufactories and showed us the number of children who were at work there, and dwelt with delight on the infinite good which resulted from employing them at so early an age. I listened without contradicting him... and returned with a feeling at heart which makes me thank God I am not an Englishman...

(The guide) remarked that nothing could be so beneficial to a country as manufactures. 'You see these children, sir,' said he. 'In most parts of England poor children are a burthen to their parents and to the parish; here the parish, which would else have to support them, is rid of all expense; they get their bread almost as soon as they can run about, and by the time they are seven or eight years old bring in money. There is no idleness among us: they come at five in the morning; we allow them half an hour for breakfast, and an hour for dinner; they leave work at six, and another set relieves them for the night; the wheels never stand still.' I was looking while he spoke, at the unnatural dexterity with which the fingers of these little creatures were playing in the machinery, half giddy myself with the noise and the endless motion; and when he told me there was no rest in these walls, day nor night, I thought that if Dante had peopled one of his hells with children, here was a scene worthy to have supplied him with new images of torment...

Women and children in a cotton factory (from a drawing published in 1892)

Robert Southey

I ventured to inquire afterwards concerning the morals of the people who were trained up in this monstrous manner, and found, what was to be expected, that in consequence of herding together such numbers of both sexes, who are utterly uninstructed in the commonest principles of religion and morality, they were as debauched profligate as human beings under the influence of such circumstances must inevitably be; the men drunken, the women dissolute; that however high the wages they earned, they were too improvident ever to lay by for a time of need...

The dwellings of the labouring manufacturers are in narrow streets and lanes, blocked up from light and air... crowded together because every inch of land is of such value, that room for light and air cannot be afforded them. Here in Manchester a great proportion of the poor lodge in cellars, damp and dark, where every kind of filth is suffered to accumulate, because no exertions of domestic care can ever make such homes decent. These places are so many hot-beds of infection; and the poor in large towns are rarely or never without an infectious fever among them, a plague of their own, which leaves the habitations of the rich... unvisited.

...Let us leave to England the boast of supplying all Europe with her wares; let us leave to these lords of the sea the distinction of which they are so tenacious, that of being the white slaves of the rest of the world, and doing for it all its dirty work."

Notes
The text is from R Southey, "Letters from England" (3 vols 1808), translated from the Spanish in 1808, II, 81-97.

Johann Georg May
(fl 1814)

In 1814, the Prussian government in Berlin sent Johann Georg May, a civil servant and factory commissioner, on an assignment to England in order to investigate the secrets and technical knowledge of British industry. During his three months in England, May assembled a detailed survey of industrial techniques for the attention of the minister for trade and industry in Berlin.

"Manchester is famous throughout the world as the centre of cotton manufacture. However, the neighbouring town of Stockport promises to become a second Manchester... Both towns are linked together by a splendid highway several miles long which is almost continually occupied throughout its length with weavers' cottages.

There are hundreds of factories in Manchester which tower up to five and six storeys in height. The huge chimneys at the side of these buildings belch forth black coal vapours and this tells us that powerful steam engines are used here. The clouds of coal vapour can be viewed from afar. The houses are blackened by it. The river which flows through Manchester is so filled with waste dye matter that it looks like a dye-vat. The whole scene is one of melancholy. Nevertheless, one sees everywhere about the town busy, cheerful and well-fed people and this raises one's spirit.

With a letter of recommendation there are no problems for a visitor in gaining admission to factories in Manchester. One sees in the town cotton mills of all kinds. In order to save on wages, mule jennies have been built so that no less than 600 spindles can be operated by one adult and two children... A child earns from 6d to one shilling per day and a grown girl or woman from one shilling to two shillings per day. A man earns from £1 to £2 per week.

In the large spinning mills different types of machines stand in rows like regiments in an army. Machine parts are, as much as possible, made of iron. The frames are now always made of cast iron because it is cheaper than timber and takes up less space. Furthermore, insurance premiums are less if cast iron frames are used...

In the centre of Manchester, where the offices of the merchants and the warehouses are situated, is a permanent trade fair. The warehouses are especially notable because of their windows which are more broad than high. This is partly due to the window tax and partly because the storing of goods in a warehouse is much more suitable if the ceiling is low. Sometimes when I stood in the street in order to read the address on some particular business premises, I was surrounded by several commission agents who offered for sale twist and calico. The Exchange at the market place is the great arena of trade. As in London, news from all over the world arrives at the Exchange."

The Exchange in 1816 (from Aston's "Picture of Manchester")

The observations made in Manchester by May were mostly of a technical nature and concerned with the construction of machines and with industrial processes. He was especially interested in comparing these new techniques with their counterparts in his native Germany.

Notes
The text is from the report of J G May, reproduced in J Kuczynski, "Die Geschichte der Lage der Arbeiter unter dem Kapitalismus" (Berlin 1964), XXIII, 178-181.

Johann (Hans) Caspar Escher
(1775 - 1859)

Johann Escher was a member of a prominent Swiss family who were pioneer industrialists in their native country. Escher was trained as an architect in Rome and he also developed a considerable interest in the construction of textile machinery. His energetic activities as an industrialist in Switzerland led him to visit England for three and a half months in 1814 in order to assess the new industrial scene and examine the threat to the youthful Swiss textile industry.

Hans Caspar Escher

"At 3.00pm on August 11 we left London and travelled like the wind to Manchester on one of the many thousands of coaches which fly from one end of the country to the other. At 9.00pm on August 12 we arrived in the famous town of Manchester. With the exception of a short stretch of rather wild countryside, the districts which we passed through were very similar. One park followed another and the remainder alternated between meadows and arable farmland. However, there is less of the latter around Manchester than there is near London. Several neat little towns, some splendid factory towns and a few really genuine villages were the only sights which flashed past us like shadows.

Whilst people in Switzerland complain about the heat, the people here in Manchester actually light their fires in the morning, mainly because it is damp and foggy rather than because it is cold. Although there are things to admire here and although I appreciate that the English prefer their own country to any other, times for us would have to be very bad indeed before I would exchange our cheery and bright climate for the dull and gloomy weather in England. All visitors to England speak of the soft green hues of its countryside and undoubtedly this is characteristic of the landscape here. However, in my opinion, this landscape soon loses its charm because of its overall similarity.

...In a short stroll which only lasted fifteen minutes I counted over sixty spinning mills in Manchester. I could well have arrived in Egypt since so many factory chimneys - which are needed because steam engines are used - stretch up into the sky like obelisks. Today I saw a power loom weaving factory which was about halfway through the course of its construction and unfortunately more and more are being built every day.(1) This factory was about 130 feet long and 50 feet broad and has six floors. Not a stick of wood is being used in the whole building. All the girders are being made of cast iron and are joined together. The pillars are hollow iron columns which can be heated by steam and in this building there are 270 such pillars. In Manchester, as in London, the dwelling houses are constructed with bricks which are actually baked on the building site itself... Nearly all the spinning mills, without exception, have six or seven floors. The attics, which are always used, have windows which are parallel to the roof and are similar to those used in greenhouses.

My eyes are all right again now. It was only the French sun and the dust from the streets which had affected them. In Manchester one does not suffer from the effects of the sun and dust because there is always a dense curtain of smoke to cover the sky,(2) whilst the light rain - which rarely lasts all day - turns the dust into a sort of paste which makes it unnecessary to polish one's shoes. Despite all the smoke which they create, one really must admire the steam engines here. In beauty and efficiency they bear the same relationship to the steam engines in France, as the English spinning machines bear to those in Saxony. One shudders at the sight of the engine piston going up and that a force of 60 to 80 horsepower is being generated. I cannot escape the thought that an unskilled stoker could reduce the machine to ruins. A single steam engine frequently operates 40,000 to 50,000 spindles in a mill which has eight or nine storeys and thirty windows. In a single street in Manchester there are more spindles than in the whole of Switzerland...(3)

How lucky we are in Switzerland where there is a balance between manufacturing industry and agriculture. In England a heavy fall in the sale of manufactured goods would have the most dreadful results. Not one of the many thousand English factory workers owns a single inch of land from which he can live if he draws no wages...

The district between Manchester and Liverpool is well cultivated. I also saw in the vicinity of Liverpool more fruit trees than I saw around London. Here people greedily eat completely green apples with white pips which in Switzerland we would not insult pigs with...

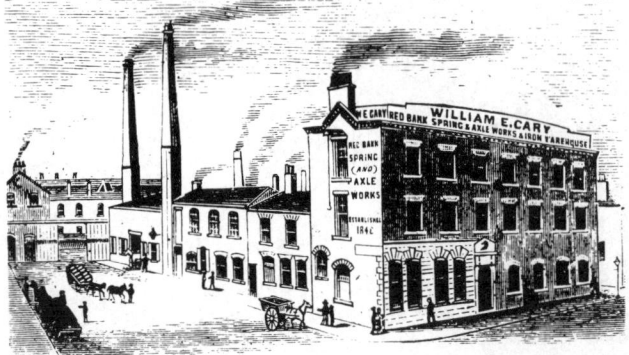

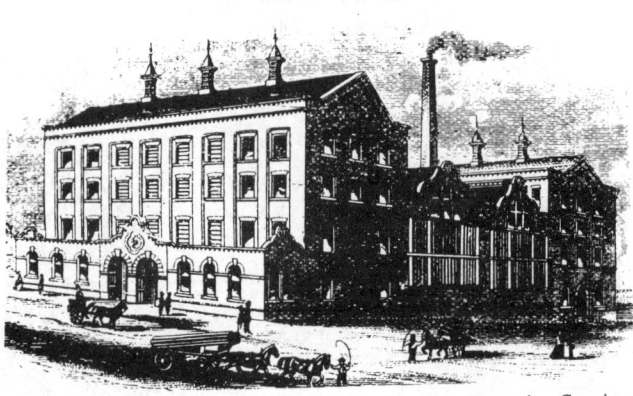

Manchester factories: Islington Chair & Cabinet Works; Abraham Nield's, drysalters; Cary's Spring & Axle Works, Red Bank; Marsden's, floor cloth manufacturer, Miles Platting

Everybody who is well off in Manchester has a greenhouse in which are grown large amounts of grapes, peaches, etc. These fruits are of better quality and are riper than ours but they do not last as long. The fruit trees in the gardens and parks flourish in a most remarkable way... It is astonishing that the coal vapours seem to do so little harm to the apples and pears...

Today I visited the lunatic asylum in Manchester in which there were about one hundred paying inmates. A long corridor separates the cells. The inmates of six cells have the use of a room in which there is a fire covered with a protective grille. Six to eight inmates sit around the fireplace on benches and solid wooden chairs. The windows are only protected by means of wooden bars. In the four corners of the room are short chains attached to the floor in order to restrain dangerous patients. Out of one hundred patients only ten were confined to their bedrooms. Almost all were free to walk around the spacious courtyard or in the corridors of the hospital and many also got together around the fireplace in the sitting room. The mild and tolerant treatment which the patients receive makes them strikingly well-behaved and peaceable. If any of them does become violent, the other patients assist the attendants to overpower him and take him away. The male patients occupy the whole of the ground floor whilst the women are confined to the first floor. I saw only a few women restrained in straitjackets. Some of the men had their hands manacled with a sort of light chain. Here, as in most asylums, some of the men thought that they were Kings and Emperors. One of them approached me and with great seriousness assured me that he was pleased to see a foreigner who could understand English and French. He asked me to explain to a French emigrant – who was as mad as himself – that he must have a new hat as it was not the custom to go around dressed in such a scruffy manner.

The New Bailey and the Irwell, 1824

The asylum was kept scrupulously clean throughout. All the patients' commodes and wardrobes are made of mahogany and the beds are very neat and clean. Scarcely half a dozen patients are obliged to sleep on straw. In addition to this asylum there is another one for poorer patients and also there is a general hospital. However, there is a serious imbalance here in that Manchester has a population of around one hundred thousand and there are only one hundred beds in the hospital. Still, sick people in the town can get medicines free of charge. Like most hospitals in England the one in Manchester was founded and is maintained by gifts and subscriptions. It is not a rare occurrence for the hospital to receive gifts of between £5,000 and £12,000. As in all hospitals, the one here in Manchester is a model of cleanliness. In this respect our hospitals in Switzerland are backward. However, the plentiful funds and the small number of patients make it much easier to keep everything clean than in our hospitals which are short of resources and have to care for a larger number of patients.

Since I arrived here I have not seen anything very noteworthy about the architecture of the public institutions. The local prison contains two hundred and eighty prisoners and is very clean and excellently maintained. It seems to me that the prisoners are almost too well cared for since they get meat three times a week and on the other days they get pea soup and vegetables (usually potatoes). Furthermore, the prisoners are allowed to walk freely around in the various courtyards. Those who can spin or weave are kept occupied with it. The bedrooms are contained in a single building which is constructed in the shape of a cross with a chapel in the centre. In each wing there are eleven cells, the

The Infirmary, 1816 (from Aston's "Picture of Manchester")

ceilings of which are shaped like vaults. The beds are good. The space of the twelfth cell is taken up by the stairs. The cells are eight feet long and five and a half feet wide. I was surprised to find in the prison a large number of youths who were aged between fourteen and seventeen years. Most of them were factory workers..."

Notes
The text is from J C Escher, "Briefe aus England", in "Zürcherische Beiträge zur wissenschaftlichen und geselligen Unterhaltung" (1815), I, 111-115 (note 1) and 104-106 (note 15).
1) In 1825 the prominent German architect Karl Friedrich Schinkel wrote of Manchester that "the enormous factory buildings are seven to eight storeys high... Since the French war, four hundred new factories have been founded in Lancashire; one sees buildings where, three years ago, there were only meadows, but the buildings are already so black that they look as if they have been used for one hundred years." (K F Schinkel's journal in "Schinkels Nachlaß" ed. A F von Wolzogen (Berlin 1963), III, 113.)
2) Escher's phrasing here is more florid in the German original. He wrote, "denn immer ist ein dichter Vorhang von Steinkohlenrauch vor dem glänzenden Gestirne." (Literally, "because there is always a heavy curtain of coal smoke before the glittering stars.")
3) A friend of Escher's, Johann Conrad Fischer, an industrialist from Schaffhausen in Switzerland, visited Manchester in September 1814 and soon realised the technological gap between the Swiss and British industries. An example of this was when he visited a mechanical spinning mill and a weavers' shed where "every mule jenny is driven by steam power and has 240 spindles. When the carriage of the mule is as far back as it can go it stops automatically to allow time for the twisting operation. Why is this still purely a manual operation in Switzerland?" (J C Fischer, "Tagebücher" ed. K Schib (Schaffhausen 1951), pp131 and 134.

Johanna Schopenhauer
(1766 - 1838)

The novelist and essayist Johanna Schopenhauer was born in the Polish port of Danzig and was the daughter of a town hall official whose family had originated from Holland. Schopenhauer's extensive study of languages included English, which was taught to her in an English colony in Danzig. Her life in that town was often lonely because her husband was frequently away on business journeys. She thus developed a close relationship with her son, Arthur, who received wide acclaim as a philosopher in later life.

From 1787 Schopenhauer began travelling around Europe. In 1803, in the company of her husband and son, she toured Holland, Belgium and England; ten years later she came to England again and also visited Scotland. Her English travels were very extensive and ranged from Stonehenge and the Peak Caverns to Blenheim Palace and the new factory towns.

Although Schopenhauer's description of Manchester is rather sketchy in its content, it contains some unusual and interesting observations. The exact date of her visit to the town is not known.

"We left Burton early in the morning and towards mid-day we arrived in this famous, great factory town. Dark and smoky from the coal vapours, it resembles a huge forge or workshop. Work, profit and greed seem to be the only thoughts here. The clatter of the cotton mills and the looms can be heard everywhere. One reads figures, nothing but

The destruction by fire of the Theatre Royal, Fountain Street, in 1844.

figures on all the faces here. The hard-working people here do not have much time to think about enjoyment and pleasure, but some arrangements have been made for them. There is a theatre here, a concert and assembly hall, in which the subscribers assemble in winter to play or sometimes to dance; and so that God also gets his share, a modern church in the style of a temple has been recently built, which, however, turned out to be rather cumbersome in its style.(1)

On the whole, the fine spirit of a social life remains somewhat unfamiliar to Manchester - as to other cities which live only from factories. Men relax from their exhausting work with a bottle in taverns; women have their own circles. However, we guess rather than experience ourselves how amusing such a group of English women might be.

The district around Manchester has few inviting features. The public promenade of the town, a kind of botanical garden(2), would not be too bad if it did not always lead past hospitals and mental institutions. As it is, however, one continually hears the screaming and babbling of the poor lunatics and, now and again, one can see them being bathed against their will, as part of their cure, in the water which flows past the asylum. This is, as one can imagine, not exactly a delightful sight; the inhabitants of Manchester, however, seem to be used to it and do not let themselves be put off by such a trifle from going for a walk on their promenade.

We visited one of the biggest cotton mills. A steam engine in the basement powers almost all the innumerable wheels and spindles which are fitted on many floors built one above the other like a tower. We went dizzy at the sight of the endless mechanical life in these great halls. In all of them we saw some women knotting together the yarns which rarely tore off from the constantly turning spindles, putting nappies on children and winding the yarn which had been spun. In one hall the still unspun cotton was cleaned; it lay on large tables in big square pieces looking like cotton wool; a number of women and girls armed with a thin stick in each hand were happily thrashing it...

Everything is done in the easiest way with machines, all of which seemed to us a miracle of industry... Everything in the factory, even the most unimportant thing, happens with admirable precision and neatness and at the same time with great speed. At the end it seemed to us as if all these wheels here were really alive and the people occupied with them were machines.

Dizzy from all the miracles we had seen, we left the building and climbed into a carriage which was to take us to another miracle, the aqueduct constructed by the Duke of Bridgewater.(3) The Duke has rendered immortal services to his fatherland, especially to Manchester, by building canals, which make the transport of goods so much easier, as well as by improving and working the neighbouring coal mines, which are, after all, the soul of the ruling mechanical life here. The aqueduct to which we now drove was the Duke's greatest triumph and it seemed to us worthy of the old Roman times.

The sight was indeed marvellous. We saw a coal barge floating along with full sail as if in the air whilst another one sailed underneath in the opposite direction. An incredible piece of luck made this spectacle coincide with our arrival at the canal. After the effect of the first astonishment had passed, we took a closer look. A navigable river flowed between two high banks; a canal on the higher ground crossed it. A dead-straight bridge sitting on three huge arches is built over the river. This bridge - God knows how - has been made waterproof.(4) It receives the canal in a bed, which is deep enough to enable the canal not only to carry barges, but ships of considerable size. A wide footpath has been left on either side of the canal. When one strolls above and does not look down, one has not the faintest notion that the bridge exists, but one still believes oneself to be on firm ground.

On the way back to Manchester we also spent some time in a pencil factory which was totally isolated. The owners did not seem to be very pleased about our visit, but due to the intercession of our Manchester guide we were allowed to watch the whole procedure... (which) was very fast and looked easy and neat."

Notes
The text is from J Schopenhauer, "Sämmtliche Schriften" (24 vols, Frankfurt am Main 1830), XV, 205-213.
1) This refers to St Peter's Church.
2) These were the Infirmary Gardens which had previously been a hole-ridden field where building clay was dug up. This field, formerly called the "Daub Holes", was converted into an ornamental garden following the construction of the town's infirmary in 1775 - the site is now indicated by Piccadilly Plaza. The gardens had as their central feature a shallow pond enclosed with a low and decorous fence. The gardens were given to the people of Manchester by Sir Oswald Mosley in 1775 on condition that the land should never be built on and that if it were used for any other purpose it should revert to the ownership of the Mosley family.
3) The creative genius behind the canal has generally been attributed to James Brindley. For evidence that the Duke himself, Francis Egerton, and his agent and engineer, John Gilbert, were the two men primarily responsible and that they called on Brindley principally as a consulting engineer, see Hugh Malet, "Bridgewater, the Canal Duke 1736-1806" (MUP 1977), esp pp 95-104. Brindley did, however, contribute a great deal towards the construction of the first English barge aqueduct at Barton. The aqueduct was built at the point where the canal crossed the River Irwell and frequently elicited the wondering admiration of visitors. The famous aqueduct was demolished during the construction of the Manchester Ship Canal.
4) The aqueduct was lined with a clay mixture by means of Brindley's celebrated "puddled clay" technique. In 1761 a reporter for the "Manchester Mercury" reassured his readers that "not a single drop of water could be perceived to ooze through (the bridge)."

Demolishing the original Barton Aqueduct; the new aqueduct is seen in the background

Johann Heinrich Meidinger (1792-1867)

Johann Meidinger was born in Frankfurt am Main and, like many others in that great German centre of trade, he pursued a career as a merchant. However, Meidinger dedicated much of his spare time to the study of geography, statistics and travel writing. From 1813 to 1815 he journeyed around France and from 1815 to 1817, in 1820 and in 1826 he toured through the islands of Britain.

Meidinger wrote two descriptions of Manchester. The first was completed in June 1820 and was published in a collection of his letters the following year. His second account of the town was penned in 1826 and formed part of his fascinating handbook for German travellers in England and Ireland; this contained much information on the points of interest in both town and country: travel facilities, history, topography and accommodation - all interspersed with snippets of anecdotes and poetry.

Of his visit to Manchester in 1820 Meidinger wrote, "The way from Derby led me through the populous factory towns of Stockport and Manchester. The population of both these towns and their neighbouring districts is incredible... Poverty and uncleanliness are everywhere apparent. Brutality (Rohheit) and immorality are rife...

At both ends of Manchester's most prominent street (King Street) small towers with embrasures had been built in order to protest against the turmoil prevailing there at

Market Street in 1822

that time. The whole day long patrols move through the streets...

Manchester is a sprawling town with few beautiful streets and buildings - mostly nothing else apart from warehouses and factories. Among the workers one sees a large number of pale and poorly-dressed people who live on buttermilk, oatcakes and potatoes. The Poor Relief is two pence per day for a single man and four pence a day for a family. This modest contribution is supposed to amount to £350 per week, therefore the proportion of poor people in Manchester would be 40,000! Whether this Poor Relief is honestly and conscientiously administered is another question.

At the end of the week the crowds at the market and in Market Street are extraordinary. On Saturdays the shops are seldom closed before midnight or 1.00am, because on this day the workers receive their wages late in the evening and then they get the remains of their provisions. Many also immediately squander their wages in the taverns, whilst their half-starved families remain at home in the most dire straits...

From Manchester to Liverpool the district is flat and marshy but very fertile. The highways here are surfaced and because of the tremendous speed of the journey, one is well and truly shaken about. The journey is completed in just under four hours. On these highways the fast journeys have already given rise to serious accidents, therefore a recent Act of Parliament made the coach operators even more responsible. The route between these two towns is very lively."

The following text describes Meidinger's return visit to Manchester in 1826:
"Manchester sprawls over a very wide area, but in many places it is still not built upon and it is mostly covered with irregular and filthy streets, which, according to the growth of the town, seem to have been laid out without any kind of plan. If one adds to this the many factory buildings and warehouses, the constant coal vapours from the many steam engines and the innumerable poor factory workers, it is easily explicable that staying here is not the most pleasant of

Market Street c1800

things to do. The new streets are, however (as in London) broad and splendid. The southern entrance to the town from the London side (New London Road) is bordered by tastefully-built houses and ornate iron gas lamp stands.

Entering the town one passes a lovely grassy expanse with a pond (Ardwick Green) and towards the centre of the town one is confronted with an attractive, large Infirmary building which also has a sizeable pond at its front. This (Piccadilly) is the most beautiful part of the town. Here are also situated the two largest hotels (the Albion Hotel and the Mosley Arms). Many hackney carriages stop in the streets. The busy main road (Market Street) continues on to the Exchange and down to the suburb of Salford. This old and narrow street was completely demolished in 1825 and transformed into a broad thoroughfare with magnificent new shops and paved footpaths, which, at the beginning of 1826, are for the most part already finished.(1)

The new town hall, a strong, imposing edifice, made of white sandstone in a noble style, distinguishes itself among the public buildings. There is also the Exchange which is built in stone in the form of a half rotunda. Daylight enters through a dome and several side windows. One finds here the best local and French newspapers and from Germany the 'Hamburger Börsenhalle'. The 'Gentlemen's Concert Hall'(2) and the 'New Assembly Rooms' (3) are also worth seeing.

The theatre(4) is unsightly and inside it is colourful and tasteless. The background of the boxes is painted in an awful brick-red colour, and at the front burn half a dozen measly gas lamps. These are made completely superfluous by the gas-lit chandelier. Similarly, the decor is nothing special and the orchestra is made up of few and incompetent players. The theatre is poorly attended and is only open in the winter.

...Chetham's Hospital (usually known as the college) is... an old school which educates eighty poor boys up to the age of fourteen years and then they are passed on to a craftsman in order to complete an apprenticeship. Their clothing consists of... blue gowns made of blue cloth. This institution stands on a cliff near to the confluence of the rivers Irk and Irwell... The college library consists of some 20,000 volumes and is open daily to the public. The Sunday Schools and the schools for the poor are numerous, but they are mostly of low quality...

Manchester also has several academic societies; for literature and philosophy(5), for philology(6) and for agriculture(7); furthermore there is a good museum for the Nature Research Society in King Street. Its collection is larger and more complete than the one in Liverpool...

The Manchester Garrison consists of 1,000 to 2,000 men (800 men are in the infantry barracks at Salford and 350 men are in the cavalry barracks in Hulme). The new Prison (New Bailey or Penitentiary) in the suburb of Salford is a large, strong, square-shaped building surrounded by high walls. It also contains the court room for the county. The prison is kept extremely clean and often numbers over 400 prisoners. Here, as in Lancaster, there are rooms with looms in them so that the workers can keep themselves continually occupied and earn some extra money. The prisoners each wear their own type of clothing; those who are convicted wear yellow and blue, the others red and blue.

The weekly market is richly supplied with provisions of all kinds. A splendid, newly-covered market hall... has been completed since 1824. Manchester also has several silk mills and a large iron smelting works."

The Manchester Literary and Philosophical Society building in George Street

Notes

The first text of 1820 is from J H Meidinger, "Briefe von einer Reise durch England, Schottland und Irland im Fruhjahr und Sommer 1820" (Stuttgart und Tübingen 1821), pp100-102. The second text of 1826 is from J H Meidinger, "Reisen durch Großbritannien und Irland, vorzüglich in topographischer, kommerzieller und statistischer Hinsicht" (Frankfurt am Main 1828), I, 302-305.

1) The reconstruction of Market Street dates from 1821, when an Act of Parliament was obtained for the widening and improvement of Market Street, King Street, Nicholas Croft, Toad Lane (now Todd Street) and Pool Lane (now Cross Street). The work was completed in 1836.

2) The "Gentlemen's Concert Hall" was located in York Street - the junction with Concert Lane now marks the site. The building was financed by public subscription and it was opened on September 9th, 1777. However, the institution never really lived up to expectations and thus it was closed in 1829.

3) The "New Assembly Rooms" in Mosley Street were also financed by public subscription and were opened on September 20th, 1792. In 1850 the Assembly

The Fruit Market, 1857

Rooms were sold by auction for £9,000 and then demolished. Warehouses were built on the site.

4) It is unclear which theatre Meidinger is referring to here. The likeliest candidates are either the previously mentioned "Gentlemen's Concert Hall" or the old Theatre Royal in Fountain Street. The latter was the successor of the first Theatre Royal in Spring Gardens, which opened in June 1775 and was closed in 1807. The present Theatre Royal in Peter Street was opened in 1845.

5) The Manchester Literary and Philosophical Society was founded in 1782 in order to promote literature and science. The principal originator was Dr Thomas Percival, who resided in King Street. He regularly met with other scientific people to discuss various academic matters. The meetings became larger and more formal and it was decided to build premises for the purpose of conducting the society's business; a house was built in George Street which continued to be the home of the society for many years. Many great scientists, including Dalton, Joule and Roscoe, were long-time members of the society and played prominent parts in its development. To this day, the Manchester Literary and Philosophical Society continues to fulfil the aims of its founders.

6) The Manchester Philological Society was initiated by Dr Adam Clarke for "the cultivation of literature in general and the diffusion of useful knowledge." It was opened in September 1803.

7) The unlikely sounding "Manchester Agricultural Society" was founded as early as 1767.

Wilhelm Diedrich Lenssen (1805 - 1874)

Wilhelm Lenssen was the son of a Rhineland textile manufacturer and was sent to England by his father to observe the great industrial changes taking place there. As part of a tour of England, the young Lenssen paid special attention to the industrial heartland of Lancashire, with its centre in the town of Manchester.

After traversing the "green hills of Derbyshire", Lenssen descended to Macclesfield and then on to Stockport, where "we soon saw Manchester enveloped in grey smoke clouds". On September 14th 1827 Lenssen entered the town of Manchester itself.

"This town with its 200,000 inhabitants has some broad, attractive streets, but all the houses are blackened by smoke. We put up at the Star Inn and found it better than in London.

...In Manchester one can find one's way about better than in London. The streets are regular, wide and provided with pavements. The houses are more or less uniform and are made from bricks without any plaster and almost all of them seem to be factory houses, of which the largest part of the housing consists anyway. The town hall(1) is one of the most splendid buildings in Manchester and is built in a simple, noble style. Otherwise one finds here few worthwhile objects of attention – other than manufactures – which we could not see until we had handed over our letters of recommendation and had visited everybody...

It was Sunday and in Manchester there was nothing to do. We therefore left Manchester at six in the morning... to travel to Liverpool and to have a look around the town."

Lenssen left Manchester on a wet afternoon on 19th September and took the coach to London. However, this journey was marred for him by having to sit next to "four thieves in chains" and a "drunken woman". He wearily added, "The prospect of driving with such rabble for a day and a night on a stretch of sixty-two hours was not exactly agreeable and I really felt homesick."

Notes
The text is from Lenssen's "Reise nach England", reproduced in the "Rheydter Jahrbuch für Geschichte, Kunst und Heimatkunde" (Mönchengladbach 1979), XIII, 48-56.

1) This was the old town hall in King Street, near to its junction with Cross Street. The structure was built in 1834 and it ceased to function as the town hall in 1877, when the present town hall in Albert Square was opened. Before the old town hall was demolished in 1912, it served as the town's central reference library.

Alexis de Tocqueville (1805 - 1859)

Alexis de Tocqueville, prolific and brilliant writer, famous political scientist, historian and politician, is probably most often identified with his classic study, "Democracy in America". However, in the county of Lancashire he is better known for his bitter and melancholic condemnation of Manchester.

De Tocqueville was born in Paris and his nature was sensitive, his health fragile and his stature diminutive. Nevertheless, his formidable intellectual capacity enabled him to pursue a varied, vigorous and distinguished political career.

In 1835 De Tocqueville journeyed to England and soon made his way to Manchester. His intelligent observations on the new industrial phenomenon of the age form a prelude to the multitude of descriptions and detailed reports of Manchester in the 1840s.

In referring to the peculiar character of Manchester, De Tocqueville declared, "The very top manufacturers are helped by science, industry, the love of gain and English capital. Among the workers are people

Alexis de Tocqueville

who arrive from a land (Ireland) where one's needs have been reduced to almost that of a savage; they can work for a very low wage and thus are able to keep the level of wages generally low - for English workers as well, who have to compete with them. Thus is created a combination of the advantages of rich and poor people, of an ignorant and an enlightened people, and of civilisation and barbarism. Therefore, it is not at all surprising that Manchester - which already has a population of 300,000 - is growing at a prodigious rate.

Other differences between Manchester and Birmingham: policing is less efficient in Manchester than in Birmingham. There is a complete absence of government; 60,000 Irish people(1) - at most 5,000 in Birmingham - a group of tenants heaped together in the same house. In Birmingham almost all houses are occupied by one family; in Manchester a portion of the populace live in damp cellars, very hot, stinking and unhealthy, with thirteen to fifteen people living in one house. This is a rarity in Birmingham. In Manchester, stagnant puddles, roads badly paved or not at all, insufficient public conveniences. All this is almost unknown in Birmingham. One finds in Manchester a few large capitalists, thousands of poor workers and a small middle class. In Birmingham, a few large industries, but many small industrialists. In Manchester, the workforce can be counted by the thousands (two or three thousand in the factories). In Birmingham, workers labour in their own homes or in small workshops accompanied by their master. In Manchester above all else there is a demand for the labour of women and children.(2) In Birmingham, only men, very few women work. Physically the working population of Birmingham is healthier, better off, more orderly and morally much more conscientious than their counterparts in Manchester."

Exterior appearance of Manchester: "On this water-logged landscape, which both nature and art have contributed to keep damp, are scattered palaces and hovels. Everything about the exterior appearance of the city attests to man's individual power; nothing to the directing power of society.(3) Everywhere human liberty shows its capricious, creative force. Nowhere can the slow, continuous, government action be seen.

Thirty to forty factories rise up on the tops of hills. Their six storeys tower up, while their

Old buildings near Strangeways Bridge

massive enclosures proclaim from afar the centralisation of industry. Around them are haphazardly scattered the wretched dwellings of the poor. All around them stretches land which is uncultivated but without any trace of nature's rustic charm and still without the amenities of a town. The landscape is already rugged, tossed, torn, dug up in a thousand places, but it has not yet been covered with people's residences. The roads which connect the still disjointed limbs of this great city display - as with the rest - signs of hurried and unfinished workmanship; the incidental activity of a populace bent on gain, which seeks first to amass gold so as to be able to possess everything else later on all at once and in the meantime simply mistrusts nature's charm. Some of the roads are paved, but most are uneven and full of puddles where one's foot or carriage wheel sinks deep. Heaps of dung, rubble from buildings, putrid and stagnant pools are found here and there among the houses and over the bumpy, pitted surfaces of public places. Nowhere has a surveyor's rod or spirit level been used. Amidst this vile labyrinth, this great, sombre stretch of brickwork, from time to time one is astonished at the sight of fine stone buildings with Corinthian columns. One may compare it to a mediaeval town with the marvels of the nineteenth century in its midst. ...On ground below the level of the river and overshadowed on all sides by immense workshops spreads a marshy land in which widely-spaced, muddy ditches can neither drain nor cleanse(4) - narrow twisting roads lead down to it. These lanes are lined with one storey houses whose ill-fitting planks and broken windows show them up - even from a long distance - as the final refuge for a man torn between poverty and death. Nevertheless, the wretches who inhabit these hovels can still inspire jealousy from others of their kind. Below these miserable dwellings is a row of cellars to which a sunken corridor leads. In each of these damp, repulsive holes twelve to fifteen human beings are heaped together pell-mell.

All around this shelter of human misery flows one of the streams about which I have written above. Along its fetid, muddy waters, stained with a thousand colours by the factories it passes, the waters are not kept in place by quays; houses are built haphazardly on their banks. Often from the top of their steep banks one sees an attempt at a road opening out through the debris of earth and the foundation of some houses or the recent ruins of others. It is the Styx of this new Hades.(5)

Raise your head, look all around this place; you will see huge palaces of industry. You will hear the noise of furnaces, the whistle of steam. These vast structures keep out both air and light from the human habitations which they dominate.

They envelop them in a perpetual fog; here is the slave, there the master; there is the wealth of some, here the poverty of most; there the organised effort of thousands of people producing for the benefit of just one person what society has not yet learned to give(6); here the individual raises himself, enfeebled in the middle of a vast desert; here the after effects, there the cause.

A thick, black smoke covers the city. The sun appears like a disc without any rays. In this semi-daylight 300,000 people work ceaselessly. A thousand noises rise amidst this unending damp and dark labyrinth, but these are not ordinary sounds which emanate through the walls of large cities. The footsteps of a busy crowd, the crunching wheels of machines, the shriek of steam from boilers, the regular beat of looms, the heavy rumble of carts, these are the only noises from which you can never escape in these dark, half-lit streets. You will never hear the clatter of hoofs when the rich drive back home or are out on pleasure; never the happy shouts of people enjoying themselves nor the harmonious sounds of musical instruments heralding a holiday. You will never see well-dressed people strolling out at leisure in the streets, or going to the surrounding countryside for pleasure parties. Crowds are ever in a hurry in the streets of Manchester, but their footsteps are brisk, their looks preoccupied and their appearance sombre and harsh...

It is in the middle of this vile cesspool that the greatest stream of human industry flows out to fertilise the entire universe. From this filthy cesspit flows pure gold. It is here that the human spirit attains complete development, and at the same time utter brutishness. Here civilisation produces its miracles and civilised man is turned back almost into a savage."

Notes
The text is from A De Tocqueville, "Oeuvres Completes" (1957) V, 78-82.
1) The German traveller Friedrich von Raumer, in referring to "the poor Irish who throng this place (Manchester)", observed that "whenever Ireland is mentioned, the feelings of the English, otherwise so noble and generous, seem blunted." (F von Raumer, "England in 1835", p226.)
2) In this connection von Raumer asserted that "it cannot be denied that the easiest labour, continued twelve hours in the day, is too much for any children; that they learn for their whole life a mechanical dexterity; that their mind remains uncultivated; and that they have neither time nor strength remaining to attend school." (Von Raumer, p223)
3) Here von Raumer commented, "The rapid improvements and increasing opulence of Manchester are very striking. Only such a city could spend above 700,000 dollars in the improvement of a single street. On the other hand, the annual expenditure for the poor of every description amounts to 230,000 dollars." (Ibid, p226)
4) This peculiarity did not escape the attention of another German traveller, Karl Gustav Carus, a writer, painter and philosopher who accompanied the King of Saxony on a journey through England in 1844. Carus wrote, "Manchester is certainly a strange place. Nothing is to be seen but houses blackened by smoke and, in the external parts of the town, half empty, dirty ditches, between smoking factories of all

Smoky, overcrowded...

kinds, all built with regard to practical utility and without any respect at all for external beauty." (K G Carus, "The King of Saxony's journey through England and Scotland in the year 1844", translated from the German by S C Davison in 1846, p258.)
5) This view of Manchester's waterways was more rhetorically expressed by the German Victor Huber, who, in 1854, described, "the reflection of the illuminated mills on the thick, black, truly Stygian water – the single small boats full of dark figures and dark bundles which here and there glide silently over a glinting patch of water." (V A Huber, "Reisebriefe aus England im Sommer 1854" (Hamburg 1855), II, 232-233.
6) In pointing out the master and slave relationship, Carus declared that "In the midst of all this is a pallid population, consisting entirely of men who work for daily wages or of men who pay the wages of daily labour." (Carus, p258.)

Eugène Buret
(1811-1842)

Eugene Buret was born in the French town of Troyes and studied economics in Paris. His visit to Manchester was part of a more extensive tour of the country – particularly the manufacturing districts. The book which resulted from his visit is most often mentioned in connection with the charge against Friedrich Engels that he plagiarised Buret's work.

Buret visited Manchester in 1840, which was the beginning of a decade of instability, economic recession and widespread distress, accentuated by the peculiar and problematic transitions within the structure and functions of the town's local government.

"Until the period of the cholera epidemic nobody in Britain dreamt of thinking about the living conditions of the poorer classes. They were set completely outside the law. Witness the many abuses which still linger on, in spite of the fact that frequent investigations have since been carried out. Passing through the streets inhabited by the poor in England, we find it difficult to believe that we are in the land which claims to be the most civilised in the world; like those mediaeval living quarters which shut their gates and forbid outsiders to enter their streets, we have seen throughout England the areas occupied by the very poor completely abandoned to the discretion of misery.

In London, Manchester or Liverpool, everywhere, we have found streets completely blocked from top to bottom with linen put up for drying – which disgusts all passers-by. We have been obliged to remove the wet hanging cloths to make way for ourselves. Pigs move about in complete freedom just as in Naples or the Orient. In these streets they have as much dignity as the human inhabitants...

The areas of Manchester inhabited by the poor are of recent origin. In general the streets are wide and well tracked, with the exception of a few hundred 'measures' along the river Medlock. The physical appearance of the people is also decent.

The streets of the poorer areas of Manchester present an aspect of a city which was once well constructed, but which has deteriorated through lack of care and upkeep.

Certain parts of Manchester appear not to have been completed, because the working people attracted by the industries had filled the newly-built houses before work was completed on their structure.

Amongst the new arrivals there is a large number of Irish immigrants and to them everything appears to be fine. They are satisfied with temporary shelter which speculators have hurriedly built to receive them. A cellar or a space under the stairs is sufficient for them...

Many of the native working families of Manchester have also descended to the living conditions of the Irish. These are the results of an inquiry prepared by a select committee of health inspectors at the time of the cholera epidemic. Out of 687 streets inspected, 248 were not paved, 112 lacked sewers and ventilation, and 352 contained heaps of refuse, filth and stagnant water. Out of 6,951 houses visited, 2,565 needed cleansing, 960 needed urgent repairs, 939 had drains and pipes in very bad condition, 1,435 were noted as 'humid', 452 badly ventilated and at least 2,221 houses lacked sanitation... The inspectors preparing this inquiry have often found two or more families piled up in a small house comprising only two rooms, one for sleeping, the other for eating and living.

Often more than one family lives in a humid 'cave', which

Outside a cellar dwelling, opposite Poets Corner

consists of one room in a foul, stifling atmosphere where 12 to 16 people are crammed. To these calamitous sufferings add the pigs and the other domestic animals with all the other disgusting natural inconveniences that one can possibly imagine. Then you can have an idea of the living condition of the very destitute of Manchester...

Yet, nevertheless, there are still in this town habitations which are even worse than those described above. These belong to the 'Landlords', where the vagabonds and people of disrepute vie every night for a place of refuge. Disastrous to the public well-being as well as to its security, these houses have not been subjected in England to a regular surveillance. The town's police force do not enter into them to catch the criminal elements. Neither the number of houses or residents nor their sanitary state is known. In these filthy hideouts people of both sexes and of all ages sleep higgledy-piggledy beneath rags and on filthy straw, up to six persons in one bed...

There is in Manchester a district called 'Little Ireland' which well deserves its name. It encompasses all the horrors that human habitation can present. Nowadays, every large town in England has its Little Ireland which swallows up day by day a vast population and, what is more saddening, some European and French towns... also have their Little Irelands. Ireland, not satisfied with poisoning England with her misery, threatens to cross the seas and conquer an empire based on famine, corrupting all the working classes of all civilised lands.

Three rivers water Manchester. Two large canals divide it in half lengthways. This is still far from being sufficient for the salubrity of the town. One of these rivers, along which are situated the dyers' workshops, presents the most disgusting view that is possible. The Bievre in our country is like a stream of Arcadia compared to the muddy waters of the Irk, above which hang houses rotting in humidity."

The lengthy quotations which Buret made from Dr Kay's well-known book, "The Moral and Physical condition of the working Classes employed in the cotton manufactures in Manchester", have not been included in this extract from Buret's text. However, it is worth noting that Buret considered Dr Kay "one of the most learned and well principled people of this land. He has devoted all his work to the improvement of the lot of the poor by educating the public in general."

Poverty: a dwelling in Southern Street, Liverpool Road, 1862

Notes
The text is from E Buret, "De la misere des classes laborieuses en Angleterre" (2 vols, 1842), I, 211-216.

William Cooke Taylor (1800 - 1849)

William Cooke Taylor was born in Youghal in Ireland and was the son of a manufacturer. After he had graduated from Trinity College, Dublin, he left Ireland to take up residence in London. In the early 1840s, Taylor was sponsored by the Anti-Corn-Law League in Manchester to undertake a study of the manufacturing districts of Lancashire. This, of course, entailed a visit to Manchester itself.

"I well remember the effect produced on me by my earliest view of Manchester, when I looked upon the town for the first time from the eminence at the terminus of the Liverpool railways, and saw the forest of chimneys pouring forth volumes of steam and smoke, forming an inky canopy which seemed to embrace and involve the whole place... Years have passed away since that morning, but repeated visits to Manchester have not weakened the effects of that first impression...

No person, however casual a visitor, can for a moment mistake the character of the town. It is essentially a place of business, where pleasure is unknown as a pursuit, and amusements scarcely rank as secondary considerations. Every person who passes you in the street has the look of thought and the step of haste. Few private carriages are to be seen; there is only one street of handsome shops, and that is of modern date; there are some very stately public buildings, but only one of them is dedicated to recreation, the rest are devoted to religion, charity, science, or business... The men are as businesslike as the place, and in their character a zeal for religion, charity and science is not less conspicuous than the buildings consecrated to these objects are in the town...

Were I asked how a stranger could best form a notion of the character of the Manchester manufacturers, I should recommend him to visit the Exchange of Manchester at the period of 'high change', that is, about noon on a Tuesday. It is the parliament of the lords of cotton... (where) very much is done and very little is said... Transactions of immense extent are conducted by nods, winks, shrugs, or brief phrases...

In consequence of the rapidity of manufactures in Manchester, the increase of population very rapidly outstripped the means of accommodation; even the factory operatives are badly lodged, and the dwellings of the class below them are the most wretched that can be conceived. This is particularly the case in the township of Manchester: its narrow streets, its courts and cellars, have been abandoned to the poorest grade of all. There they live, hidden from the view of the higher ranks by piles of stores, mills, warehouses, and manufacturing establishments, less known to their wealthy neighbours – who reside chiefly in the open spaces of Cheetham, Broughton, and Chorlton...

Another evil of fearful magnitude arises from this separation of Manchester into districts in which relative poverty and wealth form the demarkation of the frontiers. The rich lose sight of the poor, or only recognise them when attention is forced to their existence by their appearance as vagrants, mendicants, or delinquents. It is a very common error to attribute to the factories the evils which really arise from an immigrating and non-factory population; a population, too, which has been recently increased by the great demand for unskilled labour produced by the works and excavations required for the new railways which are radiating on every side from Manchester... I am persuaded that Manchester must long continue to present an appearance of great destitution and delinquency which does not belong to the town itself, but arises from a class of immigrants and passengers."

The Exchange and market, 1830

Taylor's description of Manchester was written in 1842 and in this extract the numerous statistical quotations, the reproduction of the Rev Parkinson's observations of Manchester and some of Taylor's more rhetorical language have been omitted.

Notes
The text is from William Cooke Taylor, "Notes of a Tour in the Manufacturing Districts of Lancashire" (3rd edn 1968), pp1-20.

Friedrich Engels
(1820 - 1895)

Of all the many visitors' descriptions of Manchester, by far the best known and most discussed is that by Friedrich Engels – the benefactor and right hand man of Karl Marx.

Engels was born in the Rhineland town of Barmen and was the eldest son of a prosperous textile manufacturer. Engels' father, in addition to his business interests in Germany, was a partner in the Manchester-based textile firm of Ermen and Engels.

In 1842, Friedrich Engels senior decided to send his politically volatile son to Manchester to work in the family firm, in the forlorn hope that the experience would transform him into a "respectable" businessman. However, his energetic young son had rather different ideas. He saw it as an ideal opportunity to study at first hand the effects of the British industrial revolution. The culmination of almost two years spent in Manchester was Engels' most famous work, "The Condition of the Working Class in England".

The most widely acclaimed section of Engels' book is the chapter on the "Great Towns" – with the description of Manchester and Salford as its centrepiece. The book as a whole and this chapter in particular have been both widely praised and much criticised.(1) However, what distinguishes Engels from so many other writers on this subject is his systematic and analytical approach, combined with a clear, powerful and restless style.

Engels left Barmen in the autumn of 1842, stopping en

Engels in the 1840s

route in Cologne, where for the first time he met Karl Marx. At the end of November Engels came face to face with the town of Manchester. During his stay Engels gave Manchester and its surrounding area probably the most thorough exploration ever given to it by a foreign visitor.

"(Manchester) is peculiarly built, so that a person may live in it for years, and go in and out daily without coming into contact with a working people's quarter or even with workers, that is, so long as he confines himself to his business or to pleasure walks. This arises chiefly from the fact that by unconscious tacit agreement, as well as with outspoken conscious determination, the working people's quarters are sharply separated from the sections of the city reserved for the middle class; or, if this does not succeed, they are concealed with the cloak of charity. Manchester contains, at its heart, a rather extended commercial district, perhaps about half a mile long and about as broad, and consisting almost wholly of offices and warehouses. Nearly the whole district is abandoned by dwellers, and is lonely and deserted at night; only watchmen and policemen traverse its narrow lanes with their dark lanterns. This district is cut through by certain main thoroughfares upon which the vast traffic concentrates, and in which the ground level is lined with brilliant shops. In these streets the upper floors are occupied, here and there, and there is a good deal of life upon them until late at night. With the exception of this commercial district, all Manchester proper, all Salford and Hulme, a great part of Pendleton and Chorlton(2), two thirds of Ardwick, and single stretches of Cheetham Hill and Broughton are all unmixed working people's quarters, stretching like a girdle, averaging a mile and a half in breadth, around the commercial district. Outside, beyond this girdle, lives the upper and middle bourgeoisie, the middle bourgeoisie in regularly laid out streets in the vicinity of the working quarters, especially in Chorlton and the lower lying portions of Cheetham Hill; the upper bourgeoisie in remoter villas with gardens in Chorlton and Ardwick, or on the breezy heights of Cheetham Hill, Broughton and Pendleton, in free wholesome country air, in fine comfortable homes, passed once every half or quarter hour by omnibuses going into the city. And the finest part of the arrangement is this, that the members of this money aristocracy can take the shortest road through the middle of all the labouring districts to their places of business, without ever seeing that they are in the midst of the grimy misery that lurks to the right and left. For the thoroughfares leading from the Exchange in all directions out of the city are lined, on both sides, with an almost unbroken series of shops, and are so kept in the hands of the middle and lower bourgeoisie, which, out of self interest, cares for a decent and cleanly external appearance and can care for it. True, these shops bear some relation to the districts which lie behind them, and are more elegant in the commercial and residential quarters than when they hide grimy working men's dwellings; but they suffice to conceal from the eyes of the wealthy men and women of strong stomachs and weak nerves the misery and grime which form the complement of their wealth. So, for instance, Deansgate, which leads from the old church directly southward, is lined first with mills and warehouses, then with second rate shops and alehouses; farther south, when it leaves the commercial district, with less inviting shops, which grow dirtier and more interrupted by beer houses and gin palaces the farther one goes, until at the southern end the appearance of the shops leaves no doubt that workers and workers only are their customers. So Market Street running south-east from the Exchange; at first brilliant shops of the best sort, with counting houses or warehouses above; in the continuation, Piccadilly, immense hotels and warehouses; in the farther continuation, London Road, in the neighbourhood of the Medlock, factories, beer houses, shops for the humbler bourgeoisie and the working population; and from this point onward, large gardens and villas of the wealthier merchants and manufacturers. In this way anyone who knows Manchester can infer the adjoining districts, from the appearance of the thoroughfare, but one is seldom in a position to catch from the street a glimpse of the real labouring districts. I know very well that this hypocritical plan is more or less common to all great cities; I know, too, that the retail dealers are forced by the

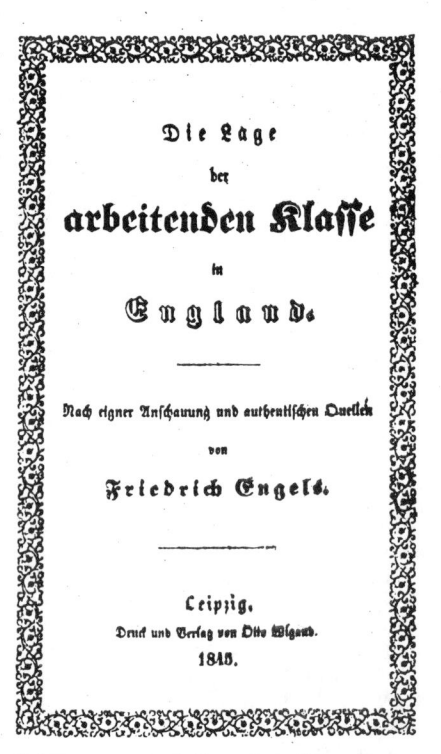

Title page of Engels' "Condition of the Working Class"

Old houses on Deansgate

nature of their business to take possession of the great highways; I know that there are more good buildings than bad ones upon such streets everywhere, and that the value of land is greater near them than in the remoter districts; but at the same time I have never seen so systematic a shutting out of the working class from the thoroughfares, so tender a concealment of everything which might affront the eye and nerves of the bourgeoisie, as in Manchester. And yet, in other respects, Manchester is less built according to a plan, after official regulations, is more an outgrowth of accident, than any other city...

(Concerning the old town of Manchester) Here the streets, even the better ones, are narrow and winding, as Todd Street, Long Millgate, Withy Grove and Shudehill, the houses dirty, old and tumbledown, and the construction of the side streets utterly horrible. Going from the old church to Long Millgate, the stroller has at once a row of old-fashioned houses at the right, of which not one has kept its original level; these are remnants of the old pre-manufacturing Manchester, whose former inhabitants have removed with their descendants into better-built districts and have left the houses, which were not good enough for them, to a working class population strongly mixed with Irish blood. Here one is in an almost undisguised working-men's quarter, for even the shops and beerhouses hardly take the trouble to exhibit a trifling degree of cleanliness.

But all this is nothing in comparison with the courts and lanes which lie behind, to which access can be gained only through covered passages, in which no two human beings can pass at the same time. Of the irregular cramming together of dwellings in ways which defy all rational plan, of the tangle in which they are crowded literally one upon the other, it is impossible to convey an idea. And it is not the buildings surviving from the old times of Manchester which are to blame for this; the confusion has only reached its height when every scrap of space left by the old way of building has been filled up and patched over until not a foot of land is left to be further occupied.

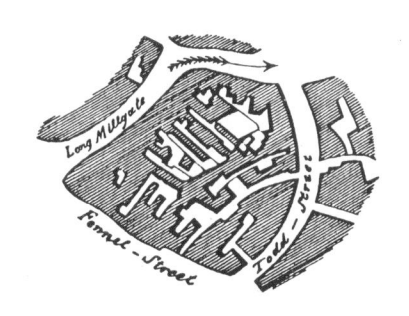

Old houses, Long Millgate

To confirm my statement I have drawn here a small section of the plan of Manchester - not the worst spot and not one tenth of the whole Old Town. This drawing will suffice to characterize the irrational manner in which the entire district was built, particularly the part near the Irk. The south bank of the Irk is here very steep and between fifteen and thirty feet high. On this declivitous hillside there are planted three rows of houses, of which the lowest rise directly out of the river, while the front walls of the highest stand on the crest of the hill in Long Millgate. Among them are mills on the river; in short, the method of construction is as crowded and disorderly here as in the lower part of Long Millgate. Right and left a multitude of covered passages lead from the main street into numerous courts, and he who turns in thither gets into a filth and disgusting grime, the

Long Millgate, looking towards the Chetham's corner

equal of which is not to be found – especially in the courts which lead down to the Irk, and which contain unqualifiedly the most horrible dwellings which I have yet beheld. In one of these courts there stands directly at the entrance, at the end of the covered passage, a privy without a door, so dirty that the inhabitants can pass into and out of the court only by passing through foul pools of stagnant urine and excrement. This is the first court on the Irk above Ducie Bridge – in case anyone should care to look into it. Below it on the river there are several tanneries which fill the whole neighbourhood with the stench of animal putrefaction. Below Ducie Bridge the only entrance to most of the houses is by means of narrow, dirty stairs and over heaps of refuse and filth. The first court below Ducie Bridge, known as Allens Court, was in such a state at the time of the cholera that the sanitary police ordered it to be evacuated, swept and disinfected with chloride of lime. Dr Kay gives a terrible description of the state of this court at that time. Since then, it seems to have been partially torn away and re-built; at least looking down from Ducie Bridge, the passer-by sees several ruined walls and heaps of debris with some newer houses. The view from this bridge, mercifully concealed from mortals of small stature by a parapet as high as a man, is characteristic for the whole district. At the bottom flows, or rather stagnates, the Irk, a narrow, coal black, foul-smelling stream, full of debris and refuse, which it deposits on the shallower right bank. In dry weather, a long string of the most disgusting, blackish-green slime pools are left standing on this bank, from the depths of which bubbles of miasmatic gas constantly arise and give forth a stench unendurable even on the bridge forty or fifty feet above the surface of the stream. But besides this, the stream itself is checked every few paces by high weirs, behind which slime and refuse accumulate and rot in thick masses. Above the bridge are tanneries, bone mills and gas works, from which all drains and refuse find their way into the Irk, which receives further the contents of all the neighbouring sewers and privies. It may be easily imagined, therefore, what sort of residue the stream deposits. Below the bridge you look upon the piles of debris, the refuse, filth and offal from the courts on the steep left bank; here each house is packed close behind its neighbour and a piece of each is visible, all black, smoky, crumbling, ancient, with broken panes and window frames. The background is furnished by old barrack-like factory buildings. On the lower right bank stands a long row of houses and mills; the second house being a ruin without a roof, piled with debris; the third stands so low that the lowest floor is uninhabitable, and therefore without windows and doors. Here the background embraces the pauper burial ground, the station of the Liverpool and Leeds railway, and, in the rear of this, the Workhouse, the 'Poor-Law Bastille' of Manchester, which, like a citadel, looks threateningly down from behind its high walls and parapets on the hilltop, upon the working people's quarter below.

Above Ducie Bridge, the left bank grows more flat and the right bank steeper, but the condition of the dwellings on both banks grows worse rather than better. He who turns to the left here from the main street, Long Millgate, is lost; he wanders from one court to another, turns countless corners, passes nothing but narrow, filthy nooks and alleys, until after a few minutes he has lost all clue, and knows not whither to turn. Everywhere half or wholly ruined buildings, some of them actually uninhabited, which means a great deal here; rarely a wooden or a stone floor to be seen in the houses, almost uniformly broken, ill-fitting windows and doors, and a state of filth... Passing along a rough bank, among stakes and washing lines, one penetrates into this chaos of small one-storied, one-roomed huts, in most of which there is no artificial floor; kitchen, living room and sleeping room all in one... This whole collection of cattle-sheds for human beings was surrounded on two sides by houses and a factory, and on the third by the river, and besides the narrow stair up the bank, a narrow doorway alone led out into another almost equally ill-built, ill-kept labyrinth of dwellings.

Enough! The whole side of the Irk is built in this way, a planless knotted chaos of houses, more or less on the verge of uninhabitableness... The landlords are not ashamed to let dwellings like the six or seven cellars on the quay directly below Scotland Bridge, the floors of which stand at least two feet below the low water level of the Irk that flows not six feet away from them."

Engels then gives a short description of the area between St Michael's Church and Shudehill. Here he admits that the housing was of a "somewhat better order", but the layout of the streets was confusing and the area was poorly ventilated. Furthermore, he identifies the problem of "the multitude of pigs walking about in all of the alleys, rooting into the offal heaps, or kept imprisoned in small pens."

"Such is the Old Town of Manchester, and on re-reading my description, I am forced to admit that instead of being exaggerated, it is far from

Inside a cellar dwelling, Long Millgate

black enough to convey a true impression of the filth, ruin, and uninhabitableness... True, this is the Old Town, and the people of Manchester emphasize the fact whenever one mentions to them the frightful condition of this Hell upon Earth; but what does that prove? Everything which here arouses horror and indignation is of recent origin, belongs to the industrial epoch. ...the industrial epoch alone enables the owners of these cattle-sheds to rent them for high prices to human beings, to plunder the poverty of the workers, to undermine the health of thousands, in order that they alone, the owners, may grow rich... no hole is so bad but that some poor creature must take it who can pay for nothing better. However, it is the Old Town, and with this reflection the bourgeoisie is comforted. Let us see, therefore, how much better it is in the New Town."

In the description of the New Town, Engels again concedes that the housing was an improvement on the Irk quarter and that such amenities as pavements and gutters were more common. However, he condemns the rows of cottages in other parts of the same district, with their "damp, unclean, cellar dwellings". Engels denounces the construction of back to back houses, which he considered "injurious to the health of the workers by preventing ventilation", singling out the example of Miller Street, where he saw courts "at least half a foot below the level of the thoroughfare, and without the slightest drainage for the water that accumulates in them in rainy weather." A description then follows of the method of building rows of closely packed cottages, which were common in the New Town area, and how the cottages facing on to the back street "command least rent, and are the most neglected."

In the district of Ancoats, according to Engels, stood "the largest mills of Manchester lining the canals, colossal six and seven storied buildings towering with their slender chimneys far above the low cottages of the workers. The population of the district consists, therefore, chiefly of mill-hands, and, in the worst streets, of hand-weavers." In reference to the many new workers' cottages in the district, Engels asserts that "All such cottages look neat and substantial at first... But on closer examination, it becomes evident that the walls of these cottages are as thin as it is possible to make them."

Dinnertime in Ancoats (from a c1894 drawing)

He explains that this was partly to "spare material" and partly because of the peculiarities of the English system of leasing, which did not encourage the builders to spend more money than was necessary.

After leaving Ancoats, Engels turns his attention towards the valley of the river Medlock and so to his famous and much-quoted description of the horrors of Little Ireland. "In a rather deep hole, in a curve of the Medlock and surrounded on all four sides by tall factories and high embankments, covered with buildings, stand two groups of about two hundred cottages, built chiefly back to back, in which live about four thousand human beings, most of them Irish. The cottages are old, dirty and of the smallest sort, the streets uneven, fallen into ruts and in part without drains or pavement; masses of refuse, offal and sickening filth lie among standing pools in all directions; the atmosphere is poisoned by effluvia from these, and laden and darkened by the smoke of a dozen tall factory chimneys. A horde of ragged women and children swarm about here, as filthy as the swine that thrive upon the garbage heaps and in the puddles. In short, the whole rookery furnishes such a hateful and repulsive spectacle as can hardly be equalled in the worst court on the Irk. The race that lives in these ruinous cottages, behind broken windows mended with oil-skin, sprung doors and rotten door posts, or in dark, wet cellars, in measureless filth and stench, in this atmosphere penned in as if with a purpose, this race must really have reached the lowest stage of humanity."

Proceeding down river from Little Ireland to Hulme, Engels briefly comments that this was "one great working people's district, the condition of which coincides almost exactly with that of Ancoats." At the southern end of Deansgate could be found the other great working class district of the New Town. Here, between Bridge Street and Quay Street and Princess Street and Peter Street, "are long, narrow lanes between which run contracted, crooked courts and passages, the entrances to which are so irregular that the explorer is caught in a blind alley at every few steps... According to Dr Kay, the most demoralized class of all Manchester lived in these ruinous and filthy districts, people whose occupations are thieving and prostitution; and, to all appearance, his assertion is still true at the present moment...

Such are the various working people's quarters of Manchester as I had occasion to observe them personally during twenty months. If we briefly formulate the result of our wanderings, we must admit that 350,000 working people of Manchester and its environs live, almost all of them, in wretched, damp, filthy cottages, that the streets which surround them are usually in the most miserable and filthy condition, laid out without the slightest reference to ventilation, with reference solely to the profit secured by the contractor. In a word, we must confess that in the working-men's dwellings only a physically degenerate race, robbed of all humanity, degraded, reduced morally and physically to bestiality, could feel comfortable and at home."

Following on from his description of the working people's districts of Manchester, Engels draws attention to the widespread problems of food adulteration. These abuses included "mixing gypsum or chalk with flour" and the mixing of pepper with pounded nutshells; cocoa was often "adulterated with fine brown earth" and "tea is mixed with the leaves of the sloe and with other refuse, or dry tea leaves are roasted on hot copper plates, so returning to the proper colour and being sold as fresh." However, one of the worst abuses was with meat. In Manchester in the early 1840s there were over three hundred butchers and, as Engels rightly points out, the supervision and inspection was often very inadequate - this is clearly confirmed in the Court Leet Records for the period. Bad and infected meat must often have been sold and, as Engels says, "when one reflects upon the many cases which must escape detection in the extensive markets that stretch along the front of every main street, under the slender supervision of the market inspectors - and how else can one explain the boldness with which whole animals are exposed for sale? - when one considers how great the temptation must be, in view of the incomprehensibly small fines...; it is impossible to believe that the workers obtain good and nourishing meat as a usual thing."

Apart from the main description of Manchester in Engels' book, there are many references to the town in the other chapters. There is, for instance, his discussion of the effects of Irish immigration, in which he relates that the Irish people, "who migrate for fourpence to England, on the deck of a steamship on which they are often packed like cattle, insinuate themselves everywhere. ... I have occasionally heard the Irish-Celtic language spoken in the most thickly populated parts of Manchester... (The Irish person) builds a pig sty against the house wall as he did at home, and if he is prevented from doing this, he

Courtyard of the White Lion, Long Millgate. Note the pigs!

lets the pig sleep in the room with himself. This new and unnatural method of cattle-raising in cities is wholly of Irish origin. The Irishman loves his pig as the Arab his horse, with the difference that he sells it when it is fat enough to kill. Otherwise, he eats and sleeps with it, his children play with it, ride upon it, roll in the dirt with it, as anyone may see a thousand times repeated in all the great towns of England."

Of all the words which Engels wrote about Manchester, probably the most revealing is a short passage which reads: "I once went into Manchester with such a bourgeois, and spoke to him of the bad, unwholesome method of building, the frightful condition of the working-people's quarters, and asserted that I had never seen so ill-built a city. The man listened quietly to the end, and said at the corner where we parted, 'And yet there is a great deal of money made here; good morning, Sir'."

The short extracts from Engels' text quoted here are, of course, only a small sample of this essential work which, even to this day, serves to remind England and particularly Manchester of its darkest years. Engels was guilty of an understatement when, shortly before completing his book, he wrote in a letter to Karl Marx, "That'll give those fellows something to remember me by."(3)

Notes
The text is from F Engels, "The Condition of the Working Class in England" in "Karl Marx/Frederick Engels Collected Works" (London/Moscow 1975), IV, 347-374. This edition uses the first English translation of 1892.
1) A useful starting point for these arguments is the introduction by W O Henderson and W H Chaloner to their translation of "The Condition of the Working Class in England" (Oxford 1958), pp12-33 and also E J Hobsbawm, "Labouring Men" (London 1962), pp 105-119.
2) The Chorlton referred to here is Chorlton-on-Medlock, not Chorlton-cum-Hardy.
3) Collected Works (London/Moscow 1982), XXXVIII, 11.

Henry Colman (1785-1848)

The Unitarian minister, school teacher, farmer and agricultural writer Henry Colman was a native of Boston in the United States. From April 1843 Colman spent three and a half years in England studying agricultural conditions. He made similar studies in France, Holland, Switzerland and Italy. On returning to England in 1848, he died at Islington in London. In the autumn of 1843 Colman found his way to Manchester. His description of the town does not leave one in any doubt as to his feelings towards it.

"Dr Playfair, a most intelligent man, is the commissioner of the government to look into the sanitary condition of the poor in the country and in the cities, and has invited me to go with him tonight, after twelve o' clock, into the most miserable hovels and dens and holes of this crowded place, to see how the inmates are lodged when they are not expecting to be visited. The government have ordered the police and city authorities to render him every aid, and two policemen are to go with us. I expect an adventure such as I never before had. He says I can form no conception of the condition of many of the poor. I thought I had seen enough. He says a great many of them who keep asses, keep them in the same room with themselves, and often their hogs, too, in order to conceal them from the authorities... I have seen enough already in Edinburgh to chill one's blood, and make one's hair stand on end. Manchester is said to be as bad as Edinburgh, and Liverpool still worse. Wretched, defrauded, oppressed, crushed human nature, lying in bleeding fragments all over the face of society. Every day I live I thank Heaven that I am not a poor man with a family in England.

I attended the large church(1) here on Sunday; the largest congregation I ever saw; I should think more than two thousand, perhaps nearer to three thousand. The preaching was dull and barren of all useful ideas...

The dialect here is the most 'gawky', for I do not know what other word to apply to it, which you can imagine. They are Lancashire people, and it requires quite as much attention as with broad Scotch to make English of it. But it would be a much more difficult matter, even if you understood it, to make sense of it. We have no people so ignorant and vulgar as the lower classes of people here. They seem to me scarcely to know their right hand from their left. It is believed, however, by some, and openly maintained, that it is much better to keep them in ignorance, lest they should be discontented with their condition...

Manchester is really the busiest place in appearance I have yet seen. In size it is not to be compared with London, but in the business streets it appears equally crowded, or as they here say, thronged. The atmosphere is very uncomfortable from smoke, and many of the houses discoloured, but the city is well-built, and some of the public edifices are on a grand scale. Trade is here said to be reviving, and great activity

The Cathedral, 1893

prevails among the works...

(I was introduced to) exhibitions of the most disgusting and loathsome forms of destitution, and utter vice and profligacy. We went into thirty or more different houses, from the most squalid to those which would not be inaptly termed elegant; and marched directly into parlours, chambers, garrets and cellars, crowded, in many cases like the cells of a beehive, but only in fulness, and beyond this I must abjure the comparison, and say rather like a putrid carcass filled with vermin. But I cannot describe my visits here, the paper would, I fear, be absolutely offensive to the touch if I should send the details. It made me very sad; it shocked me with horror, and it will make my life hereafter an incessant thanksgiving that my children have not in the inscrutable dispensation of Heaven been cast destitute, helpless, and orphans in such a country as this."

Notes
The text is from H Colman, "European Life and Manners" (Boston 1845), pp94-97.
1) This was presumably the Collegiate Church (now the Cathedral).

Léon Faucher
(1803 - 1854)

Leon Leonard Joseph Faucher was born in the French town of Limoges into a family of modest financial means. His early education was completed in Toulouse and later, at the age of nineteen, he commenced his studies in literature and political economy in Paris. Throughout his active and distinguished life his writings on politics and economics were both many and of variable quality.

Faucher died in Marseilles after contracting pleurisy, but ten years earlier, in 1844, he had travelled around England for the purpose of studying the history, the people and the environment - particularly the conditions of the new industrial towns. Faucher collected his observations and published them under the title of "Etudes sur l'Angleterre" (2 vols, 1845). He paid special attention to the town of Manchester and it has been fairly stated that his "comments on the condition of Manchester were not so detailed as those of Engels, and were more obviously influenced by the observations of earlier writers."(1) Faucher's study of Manchester was translated from the French in 1844 by the barrister J P Culverwell, who also provided valuable and informative annotation to the text.

Faucher's description of Manchester encompassed a very wide field. He briefly discussed Manchester's early history, he wrote sections on trade unionism, the co-operative movement, the evils of the truck system, the era of the domestic system, regional and national politics and religion. He also recorded a great deal of statistical information and he quoted extensively from such writers as Kay and Ure. The extracts from Faucher's text reproduced here are largely confined to his first-hand observations of the town.

"Manchester does not present the bustle either of London or of Liverpool. During the greater part of the day the town is silent, and almost appears deserted. The heavily laden boats glide noiselessly along the canals, not at the feet of palaces, as in Venice, but between rows of immense factories, which divide amongst themselves the air, water and fire... You hear nothing but the breathing of the vast machines, sending forth fire and smoke through their tall chimneys...

At certain hours of the day the town appears suddenly animated. The operatives going to, or returning from their work, fill the streets by thousands...

At Manchester, industry has found no previous occupant, and knows nothing but itself. Everything is alike, and everything is new; there is nothing but masters and operatives. Science, which is so often developed by the progress of industry, has fixed itself in Lancashire. Manchester has a statistical society; and chemistry is held in honour; but literature and the arts are a dead letter. The theatre does nothing to purify and elevate the taste, and furnishes little but what is necessary to attract the crowd habituated to gross pursuits.

In political opinions radicalism prevails. As to religious sects, the latest imported is generally the most acceptable. Manchester contains more Methodists, Quakers, and independents, than adherents to the established church...

The town, strictly speaking,... is only inhabited by shopkeepers and operatives; the merchants and manufacturers have detached villas, situated in the midst of gardens and parks in the country... The rich man spreads his couch amidst the beauties of the surrounding country, and abandons the town to the operatives, publicans, mendicants, thieves, and prostitutes, merely taking the precaution to leave behind him a police force, whose duty it is to preserve some little of material order in this pellmell of society...

Partly from the force of circumstances, partly from bad habits, home has no charm for the operative. After a hasty meal, men, women and children sally forth to saunter in the streets, or to lounge in the beerhouses. If you traverse the poor quarters of the town - Angel Meadow, Garden Street, Newtown, St George's Road, Oldham Road, Ancoats and Little Ireland, you perceive the doors of cottages open, and you are jostled by the crowd of loiterers; but if the weather be cold or rainy, the streets are abandoned in favour of the beer houses and gin shops. It is fine weather which injures the trade of the latter.

In the midst of this immense population you easily distinguish the Irish portion, which amounts to 35,000 or 40,000 in number. The English stroll in small groups, or wander about solitary, unless they have some subject of great moment to discuss, such as a rise of wages or a reduction of the hours of labour. The Irish are perpetually in a state of agitation. Often they assemble by hundreds at the corner of Oldham and Ancoats streets...

For several years the Irish labourers formed the most abject portion of the population, their dwellings were the most dirty and unhealthy, and their children the most neglected. It was in the cellars occupied by them that the illicit distillation of ardent spirits was carried on. Misery of every description, fever, roguery, debauchery and theft were rife amongst them; their neighbourhood was the chosen retreat of vagabonds and criminals; scarcely a day passed without some disturbance or without some serious crime.

Happily, however, these features of the Irish portion of the population have undergone a remarkable change. The labours of Father Matthew, assisted by the catholic clergy, were the commencement of this work of reformation amongst them. They drink less, and consequently there are fewer disturbances... But what is most remarkable, is the care taken by the priests in the education of the children. In this town where the little ones run about the streets barefoot and in rags whilst their parents are in the gin shops, and where the police take annually more than five thousand children, which have been lost, or abandoned by their parents, the catholic chapels are kept open during the evenings, and form a species of asylums, where the young boys and girls pass their time in singing hymns and listening to the instruction of their pastors...

In short, public order in Manchester has advanced. Since the establishment of the new police the streets have been more tranquil, if not more safe...

Prostitution has not, in the manufacturing districts, the same audacity and publicity which distinguishes it in the metropolis and in the sea ports... But in passing the (Manchester) Exchange towards dusk, the passenger will be sure to meet 500 or 600, and to these should be added those of a higher rank, who do not descend to walk the streets publicly... the mode in which the prostitutes accost passers-by is far less rude than in most other places. And this fact is explained by two circumstances. First, the more decent prostitutes flock to Manchester, because it is, in regard to promiscuous intercourse, the rendezvous of the wealthier classes. On this subject, Mr Logan(2) naively says, 'There is not a single first-rate house for assignations in Rochdale, because the gentlemen always go to Manchester. Secondly, prostitution for money has little scope amongst the inferior classes, where clandestine connexions are so common; and where chastity, instead of

Leon Faucher

The dinner hour

being the rule amongst the females, tends more and more to become the exception.'

The factory girls are strangers to modesty. Their language is gross and often obscene; and when they do not marry early, they form illicit connexions, which degrade them still more than premature marriage. It is a common occurrence to meet in the intervals of labour, in the back streets, couples of males and females, which the caprice of the moment has brought together. Sometimes they accompany each other to the beer shop, and thus accustom themselves to a double debauch...

The thirst for ardent spirits does not produce the same extent of ravages in Manchester as it does in Liverpool or Glasgow; nevertheless, the beer houses are innumerable; and it is there that the operative spends the few moments of leisure which he enjoys. According to the Manchester Directory, for 1840, there were then five hundred and two public houses, and eight hundred and twelve beer houses. The numerous dram shops do not appear to be included in this enumeration... To these we must add the quantities of spirits from the illicit stills of the Irish, and which escape the control, both of the excise and of the police...

From "The Bottle", by George Cruikshank, 1847

The aristocratic character of society contributes still more to this evil. If the people of Manchester wish to go out on a fine Sunday, where must they go? There are no public promenades, no avenues, no public gardens; and even no public common. If the inhabitants seek to breathe the pure air of the country, they are reduced to the necessity of swallowing the dust upon the public highways. Everything in the suburbs is closed against them; everything is private property... Even the cemeteries and the botanic gardens are closed upon a Sunday. What then remains but the brutal diversion of drunkenness?

It is not, therefore, astonishing that the rate of mortality in Manchester varies so much among the different classes of society. For the professional persons and gentry the probable duration of life is thirty-eight years; for the shop-keepers (who inhabit the more narrow and badly cleansed streets)

Manchester mill operatives, drawn during the cotton famine

twenty years only; and for the factory operatives and labouring classes generally, only seventeen years... Out of 1,000 infants in the labouring classes, 570 die before they have completed their fifth year. Those who attain to the age of virility, fall into premature old age...

The general appearance of the population does not contradict these melancholy statistics. The operatives are pale and meagre in their appearance, and their physiognomy has not that animation which indicates health and vigour. Female beauty is not to be found amongst them, and the declining vigour of the men is replaced by a febrile energy...

There are factories in Manchester which are open seventeen hours daily, of which fifteen and a half hours are occupied with effective labour. As to the children in the manufacturing districts, and more especially in Scotland, they recoup the exhaustion of a week's toil, by lying in bed the whole of Sunday. There is no order in the family, and education is a thing unthought of. The mothers, who are working at the mule jenny all day, administer to their infants a preparation of opium, to keep them quiet, or leave them under the care of the younger children."

Notes

The text is from L Faucher, "Manchester in 1844. Its present condition and future prospects" (first published in 1844), 1969 edn., passim.
1) A Redford, "History of Local Government in Manchester" (1940) II, 139.
2) This refers to the report made by Logan, "An exposure of Female Prostitution" (1840).

Jakob Venedey
(1805 - 1871)

Jakob Venedey was born in Cologne and was the son of a lawyer. Venedey's political views were much influenced by the more liberal French attitudes and this helped to mould him into a strong critic of the authoritarian Prussian government. It also led to his arrest in 1832. After his release he became involved in anti-government politics in southern Germany, with the result that he was compelled to flee to Paris later the same year. A combination of the unwelcome attention of the authorities and an opportunity to examine the social and economic circumstances of England drew him to these shores in December 1842.

Venedey's two year stay in this country resulted in the publication of his fascinating three volume work entitled "England". During 1844 he stayed in Manchester and there made the acquaintance of fellow Rhinelander Friedrich Engels, who both assisted him with his studies and conducted him around the poor areas of the town. Venedey's observations of Manchester are interesting, sometimes unusual and he had an eye for curious detail - especially of Manchester's night life - which prompted him to include in his description rare glimpses of the town's theatres.

However, the main strength of Venedey's lengthy chapter on Manchester is his astute commentary on the political scene, particularly on the Chartist movement. He also recorded conversations which he had with such prominent political figures as the Chartist leader James Leach. This work was later praised by Engels and Marx, even though their political views differed widely from Venedey's.

"The nearer one comes to Manchester, the more the district loses the character of the hilly countryside... The streets of Manchester are mostly broad and the character ranges from the proudest porticoed houses to the naked poverty of the gloomy cellar dwellings. The boutiques, the banks, the Athenaeum(1), the Exchange and the many hotels and private houses in the main streets are reminiscent of Paris and London; the poor quarter, of the poverty which I saw in Dublin. The life in the streets is almost more Irish than English... and they seem to have imbued their spirit upon the people here...

In the evenings, the street life in Manchester is about the same as in London, only more crude. ...Yesterday in the Theatre Royal(2) there were fifty people in the stalls and a dozen in the boxes. The theatre personnel along with the orchestra were very numerous. Admittedly, the performance was badly played.

The bar, the foyer and the lounge of the theatre were dominated by prostitutes who offered themselves in a most shameless manner. When I went home I encountered two drunken middle-aged women workers, who, like men, tried to haul each other into pubs in order to carry on drinking.

Jakob Venedey

The Athenaeum, 1839

In the Queens Theatre, which had only just opened today, all the seats were occupied and here the contrast became quite clearly evident. In the gallery the impudent, loud and boisterous mob held sway – street louts and rabble of all types. In the higher boxes sat young people and prostitutes who had beautiful, indeed very beautiful faces on which the fallen nobility clearly showed. They were as impudent and as shameless as it was possible to be... In the lower boxes and stalls it was very quiet and the people were well behaved. They were mostly middle class people there. Opposing characters may well be characteristic of Manchester...

Saturday night brings the happiest hour for the worker. On this day life in a factory town is the most significant and the most informative. I was already in the streets before the last hour of work had struck, and Mr Engels from Barmen, who helped me most kindly with this and other matters with his observations and studies, took me for the first time to Little Ireland and later to the Irk district.

Little Ireland lies directly between the busy factory quarter and the rich fashionable quarter of the town and it separates one from the other. It is as if it stands here as a symbol, in order to prove that England's power and England's wealth ought to be separated through the wedge of Irish poverty...

Little Ireland in Manchester is a kind of barracks consisting of about a dozen rows of houses. One has to be guided into it because... it is either closed off or covered by a factory or a high wall. If one comes to the entrance of Little Ireland one stands before a deep valley(3), in which lie rows of houses; black, gloomy, filthy, in stagnant air, next to stinking pools on unsurfaced streets. It swarms with men,

In a Manchester cotton factory

The Queen's Theatre, 1857

women and children and in the middle of all this pigs wallow in the deep filth... Most of the cellars do not lie any higher than the level of the river and whenever it rises only a few inches above its usual level, the water flows into the cellars; however, this does not stop people from living there.

Little Ireland was first discovered during the period of the cholera epidemic. Until then all the inhabitants of Manchester hurried past the place and turned their glance away from it... But cholera chose these dwellings of misery and came as a compassionate visitor to put an end to them. The rich began to fear that cholera could also break out into their luxurious salons. Therefore, the town's authorities ordered that these dwellings should be examined, emptied and cleaned. It was then that the world first discovered this hideous hole of misery. Hundreds were evicted from these cellars. Hundreds rotted alive next to the unburied dead. And the endless pestilence which was raging there had taken such a grip that all fumigation and cleaning were useless and the decision had to be made to brick up many of these pits.

When the cholera epidemic was over, the cellars were broken open and the inhabitants were allowed back. But some cellars were found to be already inhabited again. The poor wretches... lived and worked there, after they had emptied every morning through the windows with their eating and cooking vessels the water which had flooded in over night from the river. Now everything is more or less as it was before.

At the other end of the valley the river seals in Little Ireland. The water is black and dark blue and flows with difficulty over the stones which are covered with fluff and sticky with dirt. A narrow footbridge brought us back on to English soil. From here we gazed back and surveyed everything once again... In the background proud chimneys of proud factories stretched their smoking heads into the air... In front of this background were the rows of houses belonging to Little Ireland, the signs of misery and hardship were noticeable from every outline, and every stone and slate... And in the same way as the factories stretched out their chimneys into the air to pollute it, long, black iron pipes led into the water to contaminate it...

The Irk district stretches itself along the river of this name. Small alleys lead from the... larger streets which run parallel to the river, down to the water. Poor people live in the alleys, and the closer one gets to the river, the greater is the poverty...

For the last time today I went for a walk through Deansgate. ...The male and female workers went mostly in couples to their dwellings. I saw many who, despite the cold weather, wore nothing to cover the upper part of the body but their linen waistcoats over their shirts; bodices with low-cut necks, which showed the bare flesh. Many wore their bodices around their shoulders, as Spaniards do with their coats, to wrap themselves up against the cold."

Venedey here describes a scene in a shop in a cellar on Deansgate, where "many people were sitting in a row on a bench. A grate with potatoes was in front of the fire. A twelve year old girl moved the potatoes at the bottom of the intense heat with her bare hands in order to let the potatoes on top get to the fire. The child had started five to six times before she managed to get the potato out of the fire. It was a picture, a little masterpiece, and I would like to have it hung up in the dining room of every rich factory lord...

The Chartists meet every Sunday in the Carpenters Hall, where there is a very important assembly room, with a platform and a gallery, which might hold altogether a few thousand people. Underneath the gallery and above the platform are paintings and everywhere around the hall are inscriptions. ...Two pictures, the first one of Britannia, the second one of the Manchester Massacre of 1819, are hanging underneath the gallery, on which is written in big, green letters: 'The Charter - No Surrender.'

Yesterday afternoon and evening I again walked through the Irk district... In spite of the fact that it was during working hours a mob of idle louts loitered around in these streets. Lazy and mostly dirty women in rags were sitting or standing at all the doors. I encountered a mother with her baby at her breast drunkenly staggering about. Singing and organ music could be heard from the pubs. Many of the women who stood at the doors were obviously prostitutes, and more than once I was greeted by them with shameless derision. Some of these women were also drunk - perhaps never sober...

Towards evening... I took a walk in Great Ancoats Street, which is the main artery of working-class life in Manchester. (4) This street was crammed full of people. More than on previous occasions it struck me that, at every ten paces, somebody sold sweets. More than once I had already seen in the streets of Manchester a carriage and four stop at a sweet and cake seller and that the driver bought himself for a penny a piece of cake with preserves. It really looks most peculiar when an uncouth fellow buys children's sweets."

At this point Venedey describes his visits to various houses in the town where the occupants were engaged in some form of trade. How representative these comments are is difficult to say. His first port of call was a fustian cutter's house, and he declares that "The work is easy and can even be done by children, and, if one works for the whole week, one can earn about eight shillings. But there is not always enough work available. The man complained a lot and claimed that he could not live on his wage." The next stop was a dwelling where the family were employed as carders for a manufacturer. "It looked dirty and miserable enough in the house. Of course, the people were Irish, but the man was only earning fourteen shillings and his two children together three shillings and sixpence. The family had to live on this." Following on from the carder, Venedey proceeded to the cellar of a spinner. Here the family lived directly underneath the house of a rich spinner. "A woman lived with her mother and her child - a wonderful blond child with blue eyes... The woman was earning eight shillings a week. Her mother worked as a servant in the house of the spinner above

In a Manchester cotton factory

them, who gave them free accommodation in his cellar for it. But the cellar shone like a mirror on the floor and on the walls. The grandmother, mother and child were so clean that they put the rich spinner and his wife to shame... From the spinner we went to a hand-weaving family. They were English, but dirty like the Irish. Their hardship had lasted long enough to destroy their old pride, to make them forget their former wealth. Nearly a dozen people sat crowded in a kind of 'cellar kitchen'. The equipment consisted of smoothed down benches and tables and a pot with food for everybody was on the stove. The people themselves looked ragged, tattered, dirty and wild - like the worst kind among the Irish...

We visited another weaver's dwelling where a poor devil spoke a lot of nonsense and was either mad or pretended to be mad in order to get a few pence. But we also saw several other dwellings where, on the whole, we found much comfort and decency. One family was eating and, if I had been on my own, I would have accepted their invitation to join them, for the meal looked so good, potatoes and meat stew, and the people were so clean and friendly."

In his description of Manchester Venedey alludes to such familiar scenes of street life as "drunks staggering home", "prostitutes who crowd together and move into the busy streets" and people "squandering money on drink in the gin palaces". Venedey also observed a practice which until relatively recent times was common in English towns. He describes how, towards 11.00pm, the small shops - especially the butchers - would offer "the remnants of their stock" to the poorest of the people, the price of which depended on whoever bid the highest. Venedey notes that this practice took place on a Saturday night and the shop-

Power looms

keepers only sold the food which "was not good enough for the Friday market".

Notes

The text is from J Venedey, "England" (Leipzig 1845), part III, 248-329.

1) The Athenaeum was a club on Princess Street which promoted various educational and cultural pursuits. It also contained a library. The building is now used as the gallery of modern art.
2) This was the present Theatre Royal on Peter Street which replaced the old Theatre Royal in Fountain Street.
3) This "deep valley" has long since been filled in and the only indication now is the steep hollow adjacent to the east entrance of Oxford Road Station.

4) The area of Ancoats was dominated by the working class, a large proportion of whom both dwelt there and worked in the factories and warehouses there. The intense commercial activity of the district is reflected in the old saying, "Ancoats is to Manchester what Manchester is to England."

Johann Georg Kohl (1808 - 1878)

The writer and geographer J G Kohl was born in the German seafaring town of Bremen and was the son of a wine merchant. Kohl's prolific output as a travel writer was probably influenced by his family, several of whom had journeyed far afield, and also by his tutors in Göttingen and Heidelberg, some of whom had travelled very extensively. Kohl explored the whole of Europe and parts of Russia and North America in his quest for wider horizons. This point is important, because in his description and assessment of Manchester he was, unlike most other visitors to the town, in a good position to make comparisons and thus his opinions carry more weight.

In the course of writing his book on England and Wales, Kohl visited Manchester in the troubled and anxious year of 1844. His wonderfully fluent and intelligent description of the town is one of the very best that has ever been written. The account contains a great deal of statistical information (most of which is omitted in the extracts which follow) and, although it lacks the systematic and analytical approach of Engels, it is superior in its more varied content and well-balanced objectivity.

"I know of no town in Great Britain, except London, which makes so deep an impression upon the stranger as Manchester. London is alone of its kind, and so is Manchester. Never since the world began, was there a town like it, in its outward appearance, its wonderful activity, its mercantile and manufacturing prosperity, and its remarkable moral and political phenomena...

Opposite to the splendid hotel where I lodged - the Albion Hotel - stood one of the most interesting buildings in the place: I mean the great Manchester hospital, an institution offering a fund of most interesting medical, statistical and miscellaneous information. It is to be regretted that this building lies in the very heart of the town, as this circumstance deprives the patients of the very desirable advantages of spacious gardens and country air. Manchester, however, is an open, airy town; and the founders of this institution could never have guessed, in 1752, that the growth of Manchester would be so rapid, as to soon place the hospital, then outside it, within the very heart of the town...

The physician of this hospital told me that nervous diseases were remarkably frequent in the manufacturing districts. I believe there is no hospital where there are so many cases of St Vitus Dance as at Manchester. Scarcely a day passes without its receiving some persons afflicted with this disease... The most remarkable part of the statistics, however, is that relating to accidents, the number of which is enormous here. No less than 4,000 serious accidents are treated here every year. The quantity of complicated and dangerous machinery used in the manufactories of Manchester is probably the chief cause of this...

The New Bailey of Manchester, which was built by the celebrated Howard at the end of the last century, is one of the most extensive, important, and interesting prisons in the country. It contains on average, at all times, about 718 prisoners. The prisoners, however, are continually changing, and very few remain here long...

In the New Bailey of Manchester I found great numbers of boys and girls under seventeen. The number of juvenile criminals is probably greater in Manchester than in any other town of Great Britain, because the juvenile population is itself larger. More than half the entire population of Manchester is under twenty-three years of age...

The lodgings of the prisoners are always clean, spacious and airy; as for the prison discipline, I believe it is milder in England than with us. A great many of them (the prisoners) are Irish catholics... The employments used here are the same as those used in most English prisons, namely, shoe-making, the twisting of cocoa-nut thread, and finally the far-famed tread-mill...

The Night Asylum of Manchester has been opened for about four years. I visited it late in the evening... No-one is allowed to come to the Asylum more than two nights running. Each, on

The Infirmary, with fountains

being admitted, receives a piece of bread and a small allowance of coffee, which he heats at the fire burning in the middle of the sleeping room... When I visited the Asylum, the night's number of ninety was complete, and I saw the greater part of them seated on long benches round the fire, at which they were warming their coffee... Many of them were Irish, and these I readily recognised... I saw one black negro face among the white ones lit up by the friendly blaze, and I was told that a short time ago there were seven negroes here at once. Sometimes a poor brown Hindoo, or Malay, knocks at the Asylum door, and in one of these great rooms, Africans, Asiatics and Europeans often creep together for shelter from the chilling blasts of an English winter's night.

I was particularly struck by the perfect silence pervading the assembly... No-one was allowed to speak above a whisper. I was told that this strict silence was absolutely necessary to prevent quarrels and disturbances...

The same night I visited one of the Manchester police offices... It consisted of rooms, in which the police commissioners sat as judges, although it was twelve o'clock at night, and behind were several lock-ups, as the temporary prisons of the police offices are called.. On entering, the police commissioners allowed us to walk round the rooms, and our eyes immediately alighted on a dirty, noisy fellow, seemingly both mad and drunk, whose face was streaming with blood, and who was held down by force on a wooden stool, by two policemen, while

The New Bailey Prison, 1857

a third was shearing his hair in order to examine his wounds. ...In the same cell with these wretches were shut up a couple of little boys. As I approached the bars, a wild-looking girl started forward, thrust her arm through, and pinched me in the leg; she then raised a savage laugh, which was echoed by all her companions...

The number of uneducated and neglected children, who grow up in vice and ignorance, in the streets of Manchester, made me very anxious to investigate the state of the schools of this town.

Including day schools, evening schools, infant schools, dame schools, common boys' and girls' schools, grammar schools, charity schools, and superior private boarding schools, Manchester contains in all nearly 1,000 schools, and about 60,000 scholars. I myself visited only three schools in Manchester; the Royal Lancastrian School, the Blue Coat Hospital and the Grammar School.

The Royal Lancastrian School of Manchester is probably the largest and most interesting yet established on the Lancastrian system. It was founded in the year 1809, and since then has afforded instruction to no less than 24,000 poor children... Formerly the instruction was quite gratuitous; but of late years the income of the school has been so scanty, that it has been found necessary to charge a penny a week for each child. ...The outward arrangements of the school are thoroughly excellent, and the appearance of the children, although, as the director told me, they mostly came from the poorest and meanest districts of Manchester, was remarkably satisfactory. They all looked healthy, lively, clean and decently dressed...

The Blue Coat Hospital(1) is a well-endowed old school, which educates eighty poor boys at once. In Manchester it is generally called 'the College'. The scholars in their long dark robes, their lofty old church, their great halls, their ancient and wealthy library, all have a certain monastic appearance and character... The scholars are the children of poor but respectable parents, and must all be brought up to some particular handicraft...

The Grammar School is another old establishment, which dates as far back as 1520. It formerly confined its instruction to the classics, but an English school has recently been added to it..

The cotton manufacture of Manchester must, of course, be the first subject to attract the stranger's interest... Cotton is the grand central force which holds together this youthful giant - Manchester.

Chetham's Library

The factory which I visited, that of Messrs Orrell, commonly called Orrell's Mill, was recommended to me as one in which all the newest improvements in machinery had been adopted. Down to the present day the machinery used in the cotton making has continued to improve with astonishing rapidity and regularity...

Orrell's Mill is a very complete factory; the cotton is brought to it raw from America or Egypt, and it is here cleaned, spun and woven. It employs no less than 1,300 looms. These are all placed in one great weaving room, in which 650 girls are constantly at work. The humming, beating and whirring of all these looms filled the room with a noise like the roaring of the sea...

This factory is one of the best built of any; yet I found the air intolerably close and suffocating in some parts. I was also sorry to observe the terrible narrowness of the passes between the dangerous machines and their restless and gigantic arms and wheels; in these passes the floor was also extremely smooth and slippery..

There is no town in the world where the spectator may have an opportunity of seeing so many splendid machines, and machine-making processes, as at Manchester...

There are some people who find nothing but subjects of vexation and grumbling in visits to these great manufactories, on account of the dust, dirt, stunning noises, unpleasant smells, and close air... But whoever can turn his attention away from these petty grievances, and fix it on the many interesting, astonishing and, I might almost say, sublime results of human skill, invention and industry... will acknowledge that there is an enjoyment in such scenes, seldom surpassed in any place, an enjoyment belonging exclusively to this most wonderful country, of a truly wonderful age...

Among the most interesting places (in Manchester) must of course be the Exchange, the parliament of the cotton lords, as it is sometimes called. The Manchester Exchange is one of the handsomest and most spacious in England... On the evening before the morning on which I visited this Exchange, the important news from Asia had arrived, bringing simultaneous tidings of the peace with China and the termination of the Indian War. The effect of this intelligence, I was told, had been immense, and the rejoicings of the merchants and manufacturers unbounded. Agree-

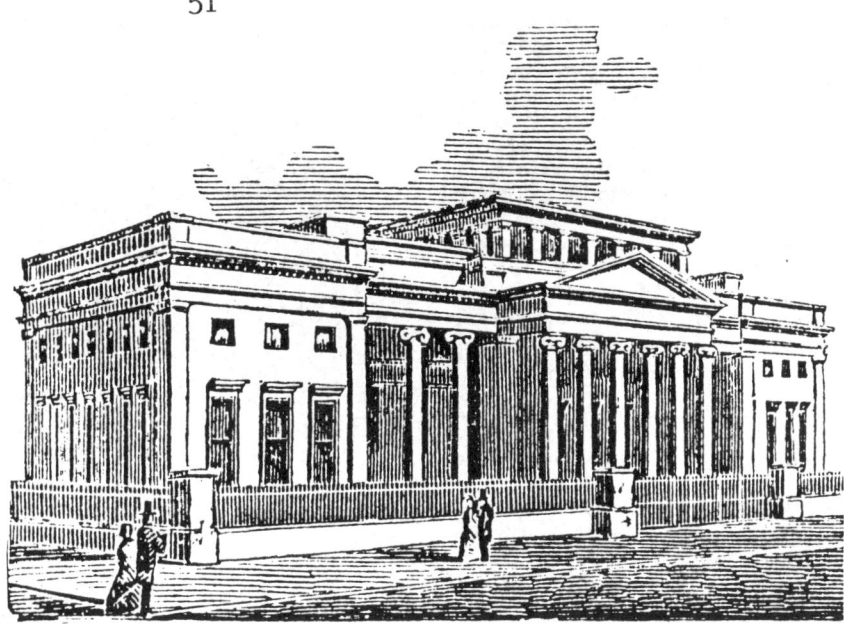

Royal Institution, Mosley Street, 1857

ments, contracts, and purchases of extraordinary number and importance, had been transacted only a few hours after the receipt of this news, upon the strength of it. I expected to find nothing but jubilee, exultation and merry faces on the Exchange. What was my surprise, however, to see nothing of the kind! The merchants looked as grave, busy and sober as ever... English exultation is very quiet and sober..

A 'Newsroom' is connected with the Exchange of Manchester... At this room are received on average 140 periodicals, English and foreign, every day... Periodical literature is that which flourishes most at Manchester. In this city are published five or six of those colossal English morning newspapers, of which the simple German reader wonderingly asks himself, how anybody can read them from beginning to end over his after dinner pipe!

...When I was in Manchester, most of the scientific, artistic and literary institutions of the town (in which it was never wealthy) were in a very decaying state. The Zoological Society was selling its wild beasts by auction; the owners of the Royal Theatre had just been declared bankrupt; the Athenaeum was fast falling into ruins; the Lancastrian School was losing support. In a place where the utilitarian spirit of trade is so dominant, as in Manchester, such institutions are sure to be the first victims of any general depression in the commercial and manufacturing world.

Manchester, like most of the other great English towns, contains a Royal Institution for the encouragement of artists... When I visited it, the exhibition contained 500 pictures, mostly by English artists. Few of these represented great historical scenes, and there were scarcely any Biblical pictures.. There were also plenty of 'portraits of dogs', 'farmer's boys', 'dead game', 'horses in a stable', and other such favourite subjects with English painters.

Manchester contains two of the so-called 'Mechanics Institutions'(2), which have of late years become common all over England. These institutions, designed for the benefit and improvement of the working-classes, generally contain a library, a museum of some kind, a lecture room... and a school for the children of the shareholders...

The Museum of Natural History, established at Manchester a few years ago, already occupies one of the first places among the museums of Great Britain... Its most wealthy department is that of ornithology, in which it may fairly challenge comparison with the finest museums in the world...

It cannot be said that Manchester is either an ugly or a beautiful town, for it is both at once. Some quarters are dirty, mean, ugly and miserable-looking to an extreme; others are interesting, peculiar and beautiful in the highest degree... (Market Street) is always busy, noisy and interesting, and contains numbers of splendid shops. In the evening, its thousands of gas-lights glittering from the shops and street lamps make it almost painfully dazzling to eyes not yet accustomed to these nightly illuminations of the great English cities. In this street the beggars of Manchester love to congregate, importuning the wealthy and idle as they pass. There in the side gutters stand the poor broken-down manufacturing labourers, moaning out their usual lamentation - 'Out of employment'. Between the idle rich and the idle poor the industrious middle classes push their eager way... Here at the corner of the street stands perhaps some poor Hindoo beggar, dressed in dirty white muslin, his dark face surmounted by a white turban, holding the story of his misfortunes, written on a slip of paper, in his hand...

Among these busy and idle crowds, numbers of Hackney coaches and cabs pursue their way, and in still greater numbers, the carts, waggons, and vans of the merchants and manufacturers, of all sorts and sizes, hurry along. On the side pavement poor girls, laden like these vans with as much cotton and calico as they can carry, drag themselves from one place to another. These are probably the workpeople of the smaller manufacturers, who, unable to purchase vans, load their workpeople in this unmerciful manner.

Let us now turn into one of the by-streets which diverge from Market Street, into Mosley Street, or Cooper Street, for instance. Here stand the great warehouses, five or six stories high, all large and imposing, some of them stately and elegant. At night these warehouses are brilliantly lighted from top to bottom... There are people here, possessing annual incomes of many thousands, who work like horses all the year round, stinting themselves in sleep and mealtimes, and grudging every moment given to amusement or society... Business is their habit, their delight, their very existence; and a place without business would be to them empty and joyless in the extreme...

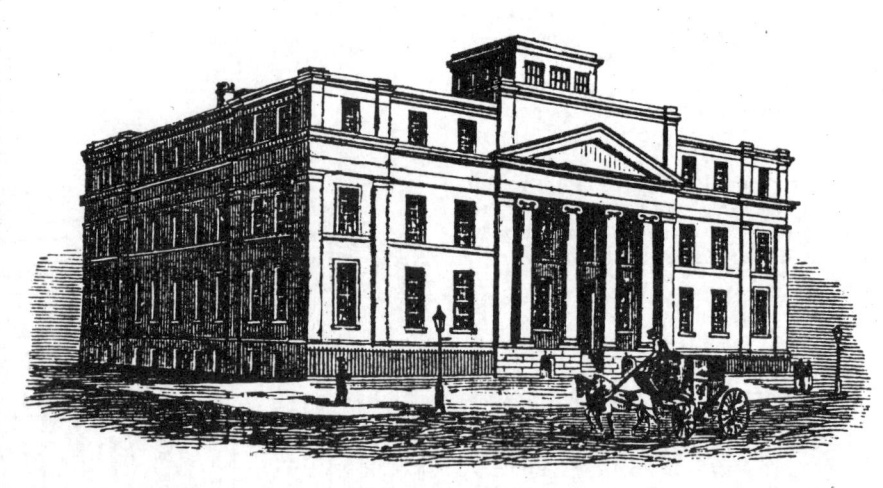

Natural History Museum, 1857

It is at six o'clock in the morning that these streets are busiest and fullest. This is the hour when the great factories begin their work and, on every side, the pavement is covered with labourers, old and young, men, women and children, hastening to their daily employments, and clattering over the pavements with their wooden shoes...

(The river) pours on its thick muddy current through the streets of the city... The blue heavens above are hidden from us by the thick smoke of the huge factory chimneys which weave a close impenetrable veil of brown fog between the city and the sky. For half a century these bridges (over Manchester's rivers) have not basked in the warm glory of sunshine; only the cold faces of the moon and stars are permitted to look upon them, for at night the factories rest, and the clouds disperse...

(In the quarters around the Irk) are the most melancholy and disagreeable parts of the town, squalid, filthy and miserable, to a deplorable degree. Here stand the abominable beer-houses, dram-shops and gin palaces, which are never without customers. Here the streets are filled with ragged women and naked children. Whole rows of houses stand empty, while the remainder are over-crowded; for in some places the inmates have been expelled by the owners for non-payment of rent, while in others they have voluntarily given up their dwellings in order to live cheaper, by sharing that of another family.

...In these miserable dwellings, often in close damp cellars beneath them, are found the poorest of all the inhabitants of Manchester - the hand-loom weavers... These work from morning till night, in close places, with scanty nourishment and clothing, and suffering grievously from privation and want...

It is much to be regretted that the manufacturing population have not a better class of amusements at their command for the recreation of their leisure hours. Gardens and promenades accessible to the working-classes are very deficient all over England, and particularly in the neighbourhood of Manchester...

Manchester is the centre of the Anti-Corn-Law... George Wilson and other well-known leaders of the League, who were assembled in the committee room, received me as a stranger, with much kindness and hospitality, readily answering all my questions, and making me acquainted with the details of their operations. I could not help asking myself whether, in Germany, men who attacked, with such talent and energy, the fundamental laws of

Market Street

the state would not have been long ago shut up in some gloomy prison as conspirators and traitors, instead of being permitted to carry on their operations thus freely and boldly in the broad light of day; and secondly, whether in Germany such men would ever have ventured to admit a stranger into all their secrets with such frank and open cordiality."

These short extracts from Kohl's text amount to barely one sixth of his chapter on Manchester, and he discussed most of the points mentioned here at greater length. He also wrote interesting sections on the attitudes of foreign employers to English workers where, amongst other observations, he declared that English workers were "universally disliked, because they were so given to drunkenness". Kohl also commented upon the youthful trade union movement and was of the opinion that "the consequences of strikes and combinations are commonly far more fatal to the labourers than to their masters. The scanty funds of the workpeople are soon exhausted, while the master manufacturers, who have often immense capital at their disposal, can hold out for a very long time." In the 1840s Manchester was the centre of the Anti-Corn-Law League and thus, like many others before and after him, Kohl made his written contribution to the subject. He stated, "The League has now, by means of local associations in all parts of the Kingdom, extended its operation and influence over the whole country, and attained an astonishing national importance. Its festivals, Anti-Corn-Law bazaars, Anti-Corn-Law banquets, and others of like nature, appear like great national anniversaries... Astonishing indeed is the profuse expenditure of labour, ingenuity, wit and talent, and likewise of stupidity, folly and dullness, with which, in this wonderful England, the smallest party operations are carried on...

WHAT WOULD THE REPEAL OF THE CORN LAWS DO?

1. It would bring down the prices of bread, butter, beef, cheese, and all kinds of provisions about one third.
2. It would increase our trade with Germany, Russia, America, and other parts of the world.
3. It would consequently increase the employment of our artizans and prevent their wages coming down.
4. It would enable the people to spend much more money upon clothing, furniture, and other requisites, and hence would invigorate the home trade.
5. It would always secure a supply of food in case of bad harvests, and of course would very much lessen the amount of poverty, sickness, mendicity, crime, and sedition.
6. It would prevent British Capital from leaving the country, to the loss of our own trade and the employment of foreigners.
7. It would restore to the labourer the right to sell his labour and buy his food in the open market of the world.
8. It would put a stop to sudden draws upon the currency by paying gold for corn in cases of emergency, instead of paying for it in manufactured goods.
9. It would destroy an unnatural, impolitic, and unjust monopoly in the property of land, restore it to its natural price, and stimulate agriculture to extended improvements.
10. It would relieve farmers, by reducing the poor's rates, creating steadiness in prices, lowering rents, and diminishing competition for farms by enabling farmer's sons to embark in trade.
11. It would increase the capital and the resources of the country so as to enable us to bear our national burdens with the least degree of suffering.
12. The rents of about 30,000 land owners would be reduced, and others would sustain losses who have leased land, expecting a continuation of corn law prices; but 24 millions of the people would be benefited, the present alarming distress removed, and, in all probability, a national bankruptcy prevented.

Every friend to his country ought to be a Repealer!

They will turn the same weapons which brought down the corn laws, against all other trade monopolies and custom house restrictions, first in England and then in other countries, until at length all commercial restrictions between different nations shall be totally done away with, and trade rejoice in the golden sunshine of freedom all over the world. A tempting object, but alas, a long and doubtful road."

NATIONAL ANTI-CORN-LAW LEAGUE. — PRIZE ESSAY — At a meeting of the Council of the National Anti-Corn-Law League, held in Newhall's Buildings, Manchester, on the 10th August, 1852, it was resolved to offer the sum of £250 for the BEST ESSAY, and the sum of £50 for the SECOND BEST ESSAY, showing the Results of the Repeal of the Corn-laws and the Free-trade Policy upon the Moral, the Social, the Commercial, and the Political Interests of the United Kingdom. The Essays are to be sent in addressed to GEORGE WILSON Esq., League Rooms Manchester, on or before the 1st of December, 1852. A letter should accompany each Essay, giving the name and address of the writer, which will remain unopened till the award is made. The successful Essays are to be the property of the Council of the National Anti-Corn-law League. By order of the Council,
GEORGE WILSON, Chairman.
Newhall's Buildings, Manchester, Aug. 30th, 1852.

Kohl concludes his description of Manchester with a miniature masterpiece which says more in a few words about nineteenth century Manchester than any amount of rhetorical verbiage or sterile statistics could ever show. "It was on a cold, damp, foggy morning in December that I took my leave of Manchester. I rose earlier than usual; it was just at the hour when, from all quarters of the busy town, the manufacturing labourers crowded the streets as they hurried to their work. I opened the window and looked out. The numberless lamps burning in the streets sent a dull, sickly, melancholy light through the thick yellow mist. At a distance I saw huge factories, which, at first wrapt in total darkness, were brilliantly illuminated from top to bottom in a few minutes, when the hour of work began. As neither cart nor van yet traversed the streets, and there was little other noise abroad, the clapping of wooden shoes upon the crowded pavement resounded strangely in the empty streets. In long rows on every side, and in every direction, hurried forward thousands of men, women and children. They spoke not a word, but huddling up their frozen hands in their cotton clothes, they hastened on, clap, clap, along the pavement, to their dreary and monotonous occupation. Gradually the crowd grew thinner and thinner, and the clapping died away. When hundreds of clocks struck out the hour of six, the streets were again silent and deserted, and the giant factories had swallowed the busy population. All at once, almost in a moment, arose on every side a low, rushing and surging sound, like the sighing of wind among trees. It was the chorus raised by hundreds of thousands of wheels and shuttles, large and small, and by the panting and rushing from hundreds of thousands of steam engines.

I went out, and traversed the humming and resounding streets, until I arrived at the terminus of the railway, which was to bear me away from mighty Manchester, with its wonders and horrors, its splendour and its misery, into new scenes, new wonders and new thoughts."

If only other writers about Manchester could have expressed their views with such beautiful simplicity!

Mechanics' Institution, founded 1824

Notes
The text is from J G Kohl, "Journeys through England and Wales" (1844), translated from the German in 1844, pp106-147.
1) The "Blue Coat Hospital" simply refers to Chetham's College, where the pupils wore dark blue frock uniforms, hence the name.
2) The Mechanics Institute opened at Cooper Street (off Princess Street) in March 1825 was the first of its kind in the country. It was removed to larger premises in David Street (now Princess Street) in 1857. The second Mechanics Institute in the town was at Brazennose Street, off Albert Square, in 1829.

W R Chambers
(fl 1850)

In the winter of 1849/50 the proprietors of the "Morning Chronicle" newspaper sent a Scotsman, W R Chambers, to Manchester in order to make a study of the industrial and social conditions prevailing there.

Chambers compiled a very detailed report on the town which covered a wide variety of subjects. However, his main purpose seems to be to defend the factory system against critics who argued that it was the primary cause of the many evils of society.

"There have been few things better abused than the cotton manufacturing system. For many years, it has been made the scapegoat for all kinds of imputed iniquities and alleged oppressions. 'Factory-slaves' became a common cant term in certain agitating circles, and 'cotton lords' were looked upon by every eau-de-Cologne sentimentalist throughout the land as Molochs and modern Giant Despairs. Silly novels aided what scurrilous and unfair pamphlets had begun... But out of all this slough of prejudice and error, the Cotton Metropolis has of late been steadily rising. No amount of folly or misrepresentation could ultimately prevent that... Much of the popular distaste for the manufacturing districts possibly arose from the ugliness and smokiness of the town; and in this respect, no doubt, Manchester and its compeers might be greatly improved... As it is, the transition from the rural to the cotton districts is, it must be confessed, not pleasant...

In the general aspect of the town (Manchester), a very important part is played by sombre, silent streets, which principally consist of warehouses - many of them of stately and symmetric aspect, with long, pillared facades and ornamented frontages... But wherever you take your station in Manchester you are not far from heaps of mean, two-storeyed houses, extending in ramifications of monotonous and uninteresting streets, and every now and then interrupted by the vast sweep of brick wall, the half dozen tiers of square windows, and towering shafts of the genius loci - the cotton mill.

In Manchester streets, there is a total absence of loungers. Busy as London is, the cotton capital is still busier. The upper class of the population go buzzing from warehouse to warehouse, and bank to bank, and office to office. At certain hours, swarms of mechanics, in their distinguishing fustian, seem to burst from concealed receptacles; and mingled with them appear the factory operatives, the true working-people of Manchester; the men, in general, under-sized and sallow looking; the girls and women also somewhat stunted and pale, but smart and active, with dingy dresses, and dark shawls wreathed around their heads, abundantly speckled with flakes of cotton wool...

Both in its industrial and architectural features, Manchester may be divided into three great regions. The central of these, lying around the civic heart – the Exchange... is the grand district of warehouse and counting rooms... there the actual business of buying and selling is carried on; there are banks, offices and agencies innumerable. The far outskirts of the city, again, form a species of universally stretching west or fashionable end... Thither fly all who can afford to live out of the smoke. There you will find open, handsome squares, and shewy ranges of crescents, and rows, and miles of pleasant villas peeping out from their shrubberied grounds. Between these two regions – between the dull stacks of warehouses and the snug airy dwellings of the suburbs – lies the great mass of smoky, dingy, sweltering and toiling Manchester. It is from that mid-region that the tall chimneys chiefly spring; and it is beneath these – stretching in a network of inglorious-looking, but by no means universally miserable streets, from mill to mill, and factory to factory – we find the homes of the spinners and weavers, whose calicoes are spread abroad over three parts of the garment-wearing globe.

The different regions of working Manchester present, however, very different degrees of architectural and sanitary progress. The old parts of the town are the worst; the new portions laid out for the working-classes are the best; and suburbs are being projected in a style which will leave all behind that has yet been done. The oldest and worst working district of Manchester is the region known as Ancoats... Ancoats, in fact, is... Manchester ere sanitary improvement and popular education had raised and purified its general and social condition. Many of its streets, particularly that great thoroughfare called the Oldham Road, are magnificent in their vast proportions; but the thousands of by-lanes and squalid courts, the stacked-up piles of undrained and unventilated dwellings, swarm with the coarsest and most dangerous portions of the population. Here the old and inferior mills abound; here the gin palaces are the most magnificent, and the pawn shops the most flourishing; here, too, the curse of Lancashire – the 'low Irish' – congregate by the thousands; and here principally abound the cellar dwellings, and the pestilential lodging houses, where thieves and vagrants of all kinds find shares of beds in underground recesses for a penny and twopence a night. (In the township of Chorlton-on-Medlock) there is a decided improvement. The houses of the operatives in all the quarters are two-storeyed; but in Chorlton the principles of ventilation and the regards of domestic convenience have been to some degree provided for. The streets are far cleaner, the dwellings are not so closely packed together, and they are somewhat larger than those in Ancoats. Here, too, 'cellar houses' are less frequent; the basement storey being put to the more legitimate use of storing coal, than of lodging, in its damp recesses, human beings. But of all the toiling portions of the city, the district of Hulme – the last built – is the most gratifying. Here the houses outstrip those of Chorlton, as the latter do those of Ancoats..

(In Manchester's cotton mills) the amount of physical labour – that is the actual expenditure of physical energy and strength demanded in a cotton mill – is really very trifling. The engine is the real worker... At all events, Manchester cotton operatives at work have very little of the woebegone and slave-gang appearance frequently ascribed to them. Let us follow them in a day's toil, and note their appearance and their habits. Somewhere about five o'clock am, the 'knockers-up' are at work. ...Many 'knockers up' have a very decent body of clients, and they make their rounds so as to give the last visited time to be ready by the first peal of the factory bell... The streets leading to the mills are thronged with men, women and children flocking to their labour. They talk and laugh cheerily together. The girls keep, as usual, in groups, with their shawls round their head; and early breakfast parties assemble at the stalls of peripatetic vendors of hot coffee and cocoa...

Breakfast hour comes round at half past eight o'clock. The engine stops to the minute, and the streets are again crowded with those of the workpeople whose homes are in the vicinity. A large proportion, however, breakfast in the factory... The meal generally consists of coffee, with plenty of bread and butter, and in many cases a slice of bacon. At five minutes to nine o'clock the bell again rings, and at nine the engine starts. The work goes on with the most perfect method and order. There is little if any talking, and there seems little disposition to talk... The mill costume is, as may be imagined, something of the slovenliest. The men wear blue and striped shirts, unbraced trousers, and slippers; the women very generally envelop themselves in coarse pinafores and loose jackets, tying round the throat. The spinners and piecers... frequently go about their work barefoot... Little enough, indeed, can be said for the cleanliness of the workpeople; they have an essentially grey look, as if water would run off them as off a duck's back...

In respect to the physical appearance and development, the cotton operatives occupy a sort of middle and negative position. To say that they are decidedly stunted is going too far; but they are certainly neither a robust nor well-made generation. They do not look actually ill, but they have no appearance of what is called rude health. They are spare, and certainly undersized. At the same time, their movements

Poverty

are quick and easy, and there is no sign of weariness or languor either in face or limbs. The hue of the skin is perhaps the least favourable characteristic. The faces which surround you in a factory are for the most part lively in character, but cadaverous, and overspread by a sort of unpleasant greasy pallor. Now and then, a girl may be observed with some indications of roses in her cheeks; but such cases are exceptional; and among the elder and matronly women there are none. Altogether there can be no doubt that factory-life does not tend to develop the frame in all its robustness, or the health in all its vigour, but neither does it seriously keep down the energies, or necessarily shorten life...

In Manchester, all the world, master and man, dine at one o'clock. From one to two, the industrial population – from the millionaire factory proprietor to the little scavenger who earns his weekly half-crown – are all occupied in the pleasant process. Offices, warehouses, factories are alike deserted... A favourite popular dish is 'potato pie' – a substantial pasty made of meat and potatoes, with a formidably thick roofing of doughy paste...

Manchester, unfortunately, holds a high, nearly the highest, place in the melancholy returns of national mortality which are every year issued with their boding columns of figures from Somerset House. The average number of yearly deaths in English towns is about 1 in 45, but... in Manchester, one individual is buried out of every thirty. From this grim fact, the theory that death and cotton manufacture go together has been somewhat illogically deduced. The fact is, that death and crowded and ill-built towns – that death and the remediable abuses of cotton manufacture – only go together.

Mule Room

...The greater part of the quota of Manchester's extra and removable mortality is, however, as we have hinted, made up of children's deaths. It is before the juvenile portion of the population begin to work in the factory, not after it, that the system exposes them to the greatest danger. It is a melancholy, but an undoubted fact, that out of every one hundred deaths in Manchester, very nearly one half – 48 and a fraction – are those of children under five years of age... Marriages in Manchester are frequently contracted at a very early age, long before the man has any chance of holding the better-paid class of situations in the factory and the result is, that the wife, like himself, is obliged to continue her daily toil in the mill, even after she has a young family growing up around her. From this necessity comes the curse of the cotton towns – the dosing of children with opium to keep them quietly asleep at home or at nurse, until the return of their mothers in the evening... As may well be supposed, the system of infant neglect continues even after the children have got too old to be left all day in the cradle. Then they wander forth into the streets, running the risk of all manner of accidents, and so frequently going astray, that the police have actually to find out the domiciles of upwards of 4,000 'lost' children per annum...

The effect of laudanum upon the children is to produce suffusion of the brain and a whole tribe of glandular and mesenteric disorders. The child sinks into a low torpid state, and wastes away to a skeleton, the stomach alone preserving its protuberance. If it survives, it is more or less weakly, and stunted for life – the complexion never assumes a healthy hue, and the vital powers never attain their natural force and vigour. The liquid principally used is a drug common enough through all the country, and well known as 'Godfrey's cordial'. In Manchester, 'Godfrey', as the term is generally abbreviated, is a household word...

It is not generally known that a favourite pursuit of the Manchester operative, when a holiday enables him to indulge in it, is botanising. The people have a peculiar taste for the

Dinner time

study; and collections of plants and herbals, arranged with no mean skill, are very often to be found among the most prized articles of the household. Zoology and entomology are also studied; the city-pent and smoke-dried people appearing to turn with a natural longing to anything which reminds them of nature and her productions.. Mathematics is another branch of study considerably in vogue among the more thinking of the working people... Music is another favourite amusement of the Lancashire cotton population. The county has produced very fine voices, particularly sopranos; and the people seem to have an inborn relish for vocal music, with a peculiar capability for part-singing...

In Manchester, however, the popular taste is certainly not so highly cultivated; and the musical saloons, in which drink is as much looked after as melody and harmony, are not amongst the most promising of the popular places of amusement... One of the principal and most favoured is the Apollo Saloon, in the London Road. The spectacle to be seen in its vicinity, about nine o'clock on a Saturday night, is not a thing to be missed by visitors of Manchester. The London Road is a vast thoroughfare intersecting a purely operative portion of the town. It is noted for its cheap shops, and the extraordinary variety of articles which can be procured from its general dealers. On Saturday night, however, the street takes completely the aspect of a fair. The broad pavements are crammed with stalls, heaped with cheap eatables, animal and vegetable, with household matters, and with coarse articles of attire. Great streams of unprotected gas flicker over the booths, and similar pennons blaze at the doors of every shop. The crowd is vast. All working Manchester seems to have assembled for the purpose of laying in its Sunday provisions; and the gabbling din of the universal chaffering mingles with the cries of the stall-keepers proclaiming the quality of their goods, the shouts of the drivers of vehicles coming slowly through the crowd, and the laughing screams of bands of mill girls calling out to each other, and joking with their friends. You can hardly make your way into a shop; and the public houses are streaming with light, and literally choked with customers, while the swinging doors of the pawnbrokers have no moment of rest. Through this chaos of buying and selling, of pushing and struggling, you make your way to the illuminated sign of the Apollo Saloon... Mounting a broad yet steep staircase, you suddenly emerge into a long, narrow room from which, as the doors open, will burst upon you a suffocating volume of tobacco smoke, a bewildering glare of light, a babel of tongues, and a confused vision of a crammed together assemblage of working men and women - the men smoking, and the men and women drinking from every species of vessel - glass, pewter and stoneware... At the top of the room is an absurdly small theatre... The orchestra beneath consists perhaps of two or three fiddles and a piano... The musical part of the performance consists very often of Ethiopian serenaders, of whom the people never appear to tire; of local songs in local dialect, sung in character; with an occasional common-place sentimental ditty, while sometimes there occurs a song not of the most decorous character.

Dancing is much relished, and all sorts of hornpipes are the staple performances... The company who assist at these performances are almost entirely mill-hands and mechanics... Everybody is in working dress, and, as might be expected, a general atmosphere of decided free-and-easiness reigns over the assembly...

The literature of the Lancashire operatives might be much altered for the better... Upon their shelves will be found masses of penny novels, and comic song, and dream and recitation books, jumbled with sectarian pamphlets and democratic essays. Cheap educational works, too, in great variety, are accompanied by cheap reprints of American tales... it is to be hoped that the reading tastes of the people will not always continue at their present low ebb. That there is a dire mass of ignorance in the population is a too evident fact. The reports of the Educational Commissioners supply the most startling details upon the subject, but the work of instruction is now making distinct inroads upon the waste...

(Irish people), when located in England, seem to acquire a strange Bedouin taste for irregular wanderings... When not travelling, the Irish invariably herd together. The

Interior of the Exchange at the time of Queen Victoria's visit

mill hands never associate with them, and generally look upon them in the light of helots or pariahs... Next to the Irish in social degradation are, probably, the few scattered cotton handloom weavers, who still, more or less, by the help of the parish, manage to pursue their antiquated toil... They seem a meek and long-suffering race, acknowledging that the world has gone by them, but still obstinately refusing to follow in the track, and driving the weary shuttle disconsolately on, while steam drives scores of thousands at twenty times the speed...

The place to see the assembled industrial aristocracy of Manchester is on the Exchange upon Tuesdays at noon. Then it is High 'Change. In the magnificent pillared hall move, almost like so many phantoms, a crowd of keen, anxious-looking men; portly, sixteen stone personages, with rosy cheeks, but with none of the vacant, aldermanic look about them; sallow Yankees, tall and lank, with oddly shaped hats, and particularly well got up about the boots; bustling agents, full of civility, and eager to do a bargain; and sharp Exchange clerks, who come to represent their employers' houses. The taciturnity of the crowd at first strikes you. You hear no vacant gossiping, no laughing, no loud talking whatever; yet an electric stream of intelligence seems to pervade the whole assembly, and everyone by a look, a gesture, perhaps with a muttered word or two, appears to make himself fully understood. Now, what does all the whispering, and nodding, and winking mean? Why don't they speak out? Why, because they are doing business - sounding each other, to an amount of money that would appear fabulous. Hundreds of thousands of pounds change hands in these broken words and unfinished sentences. A cotton sale is soon effected. You may catch the words: 'Brand', 'Ex Mary Jane', 'Bales', 'Three thousand pounds', 'Eh?', 'Yes', 'Well done', and the agreement is concluded."

Also included in Chambers' report were comparisons between the housing in the older district of Ancoats and the newer district of Hulme; descriptions of some of the textile processes; an outline of the different types of cotton mills; recent improvements in industrial technology and social reform; a variety of statistical quotations - especially on the question of mortality; the effects of the then recent Ten Hours Bill which restricted the hours of labour for a worker in a cotton mill; and a brief discussion of the relationship between Manchester and its satellite towns. Chambers went into all of these and the other points in greater detail than is suggested by the extracts reproduced here.

Chambers concludes his admirable description of Manchester by asserting his belief in one of the fundamental principles of the capitalist philosophy: "The workpeople are beginning to see that no law prevents them from aspiring and attaining to the rank of capitalists themselves. There is no want of examples of the feat being performed; many of the Manchester mill owners have originally been mill hands; and, in the industrial career opened up to the producing regions of the north by our recent commercial revolution, it is to be hoped that the opportunity will be presented to many a young operative of rivalling the achievements of those who have gone before him, and of raising himself - through the agencies of industry, probity, and intelligence - from the frame and the loom to the counting house and the Exchange."

Notes
The text is from W R Chambers, "The Cotton Metropolis", originally from a report in the "Morning Chronicle". Reprinted and published in 1972.

Queen Victoria
(1819 - 1901)

On the afternoon of October 10th 1851 Queen Victoria became the first English monarch to visit Manchester. The town's authorities and many leading industrialists were anxious that their Sovereign should receive the most favourable impression of the great commercial capital. There was, therefore, a period of intense activity for several weeks prior to the visit whilst elaborate preparations were made. Over one hundred and fifty workmen were employed to construct a set of fountains at the Infirmary Pond at Piccadilly. (The site of the pond is indicated today by Piccadilly Gardens.) There were also two highly ornate "triumphal arches" constructed on the newly named Victoria Bridge (the successor of Old Salford Bridge) and on Albert Bridge, at a cost of £300 each; these arches were demolished after the Royal visit. The town council also decided on "illuminating the town hall and also the Exchange by large and splendid devices in gas and cut-glass".(1) A double triumphal arch was built to span St Ann's Square and the square itself was illuminated by four thousand oil lamps. The construction of a "magnificent throne" for Her Majesty's pleasure in the Exchange entailed the removal of four

The Infirmary and fountains at the time of Victoria's visit to Manchester

supporting stone columns by workmen who laboured in continuous shifts for fifteen days. Most significant of all was that "Various streets have been newly paved for the occasion; and the painting and cleansing of the exteriors of buildings has been very general throughout the streets included in the Royal route. Hordes and fences have been removed; ugly obstructions got rid of and there has been generally a strong desire and effort to make Manchester put on its best face to greet its Sovereign." Thus the scene was set for the eagerly awaited arrival.

After visiting Liverpool, the Queen and the Prince Consort stayed at Worsley. On Friday October 10th they journeyed to Pendleton and then into Salford, where they were met by huge crowds. The Queen wrote in her diary, "The day was fine and mild, and everything to a wish ... we first came to Pendleton, where, as everywhere else, there are factories, and great preparations were made. School-children were there in profusion. We came next to Salford, where the crowd became very dense...

The mechanics and workpeople, dressed in their best, were ranged along the streets, with white rosettes in their button-holes; both in Salford and Manchester, a very intelligent, but painfully unhealthy-looking population(2) they all were, men as well as women... All the children sang 'God Save the Queen' extremely well together..

We passed... through the principal street of Salford, on to Manchester, at the entrance of which was a magnificent arch. The Mayor, Mr Potter(3), who went through the proceedings with great composure and self-possession, beautifully dressed, (the Mayor and Corporation had until now been too radical to have robes)(4) received us there, and presented me with a beautiful bouquet. We drove through the principal streets, in which there are no very fine buildings – the principal large houses being warehouses – and stopped at the Exchange(5), where we got out and received the Address again on a throne, to which I read an answer. The streets were immensely full, and the cheering and enthusiasm most gratifying. The order and good behaviour of the people, who were not placed behind any barriers, were the most complete we have seen in our many progresses through capitals and cities... Nobody moved, and therefore everybody saw well, and there was no squeezing... We returned as we came, the sun shining brightly, and were at Worsley by two."

After her return to Worsley, the Queen further penned in her diary that "The Mayor (now Sir John Potter, he having been knighted after presenting the Manchester address) told me last night, that he thinks we saw a million of people between Manchester and Salford. There are 400,000 inhabitants in Manchester, and everyone says, that in no other town could one depend so entirely upon the quiet and orderly behaviour of the people as in Manchester. You had only to tell them what ought to be done and it was sure to be carried out."

After departing from the rural surrounds of Worsley, the Royal party again "went through Manchester, and had an opportunity of seeing the extraordinary number of warehouses and manufactories it contains, and how large it is." The royal visitors passed through Stockport on their way back to Windsor.

Extract from Princess Beatrice's copy of the Queen's diary, commenting on Mayor John Potter

Outside the Exchange at the time of Victoria's visit, 1851

Notes
The text is from the diary of Queen Victoria, reproduced in T Martin, "Life of the Prince Consort" (1876), II, 399-402. The original diary is not known to exist, but a copy was

Henry Adams
(fl 1861)

During the mid-nineteenth century there was an increasing trend in the northern manufacturing areas of the United States towards a protectionist trade policy which was strongly resented by the more agricultural south. The southern states largely depended on slave labour for cotton, tobacco and sugar. The northern opponents of slavery succeeded in securing a majority to abolish slavery and this led to an attempt by the south to break away from the Union. The very existence of the United States was thereby seriously threatened and the result was civil war.

The appalling human loss caused by this senseless war tends to be overshadowed in English histories by the commercial loss of the Lancashire textile industry. The main source of raw cotton for Lancashire was the southern states of America and thus when the north imposed its blockade, Lancashire was almost drained of its life-blood. (1) The distress among the Lancashire workforce was devastating. Unlike the factory owners, the operatives had little or no money to fall back on and thus many relief agencies were quickly established. However, bankruptcy awaited many Manchester factory owners too, and no fewer than 1,193 went out of business between 1861 and 1864. Yet there was scarcely any violence among the distressed, unemployed operatives; indeed, they were frequently praised for their patience and fortitude.(2)

In November 1861 a twenty-three year old American, Henry Adams, arrived in Manchester from London. His main purpose in visiting the town was to ascertain the attitudes and opinions of the textile concerns towards the blockade of the southern states by the north. He came away firmly convinced that support for the blockade was widespread in Manchester. Aside from these considerations, Adams made some other interesting observations on the town.

"It is a peculiarity of these manufacturing places, that if one really wishes to see them, one must go out of them. The city of Manchester seems to be a collection of enormous warehouses, banks and shops, set in a broad margin of common brick houses, which the lower classes live in. But the best and largest factories lie at a distance varying from one mile to fifty or thereabouts, in little towns of their own, and the houses of the wealthy citizens are all country houses on the outskirts of the town, so that for miles about one meets long and very pretty roads lined with villas and parks, which make the environs charming, but which leave the city proper very dull and gloomy, from the want of handsome private houses. As we entered the streets, the sun, which had been shining brightly two miles away, became a dull red ball in the smoke and fog, and no one who was not accustomed to the atmosphere would have supposed that it was a fine day(3)...

Manchester society seems to be much more like what one finds in American cities than like that of London. In Manchester as in America it seems to have fallen, or be falling, wholly into the hands of the young, unmarried people. In London the court gives it dignity and tone, and the houses into which an admission is thought of most value, are generally apt to slight dancing. In Manchester, I am told, it is still the fashion for the hosts to see that their guests enjoy themselves. In London the guests shift for themselves, and a stranger had better depart at once as soon as he has looked at the family pictures. In Manchester one is usually allowed a dressing room at an evening party. In London a gentleman has to take his chance of going into the little ballroom with his hair on end or his cravat untied. In Manchester it is still the fashion to finish balls with showy suppers, which form the great

---

1857: Sir John Potter is still capitalising on the Queen's approval in this election advertisement!

made by Queen Victoria's daughter, Princess Beatrice. This copy differs slightly from the account quoted by Theodore Martin, and as Martin also had access to the original journal it is difficult to decide which version is the more accurate. The points where Princess Beatrice's copy differs from Martin's text are indicated in the footnotes.

1) This and the following quotation are from an article in the "Manchester Guardian", 11th October 1851.
2) The copy by Princess Beatrice here reads "a very intelligent but painfully unhealthy and sickly population".
3) Princess Beatrice wrote here that "The Mayor, Mr Potter, a young, tall, very fair and 'debonaire' looking man got through the whole with great composure and self-possession."
4) The then recently formed Manchester Borough Council had refused to allow the use of civic robes, but Sir John Potter personally initiated their introduction specially for the occasion of the Queen's visit, and they have remained ever since.
5) Following Queen Victoria's visit to Manchester, a request was made to designate the Exchange "The Manchester Royal Exchange". This met with the approval and consent of the Queen.

Henry Adams

test of the evening period. In London one is regaled with thimbles full of ice cream and hard seed cakes. I presume the same or similar differences run through all the great provincial towns. London society is a distinct thing, which the provinces are sensible not to try to imitate...

(In a Manchester cotton mill) the operatives were dirty, very coarsely dressed, and very stupid in looks; altogether much inferior to the American standard. About a quarter of the spindles were silent, and, as they told me, a corresponding number of the operatives discharged, to starve as they best might...

As yet, we need fear no active hostility from Manchester, but so soon as the mills can again be worked at a profit, difficulty and a hot contest may be expected, which will grow intense in proportion as the prospect of money-making increases. But in spite of their present assertions I think that in such a case the radicals, the anti-slavery interests, and the colonies, would unite in preferring a prohibitive duty, if necessary, to a war."

Notes

The text is from Henry Adams' "Diary of a Visit to Manchester", originally in the "Boston Courier" of 16th December 1861 and reproduced in A W Silver, "Henry Adams' Diary of a Visit to Manchester", in the "American Historical Review", LI (Oct 1945) 74-89.

1) A journalist from "The Times" visited Manchester in 1862 and informed his readers that "We are bold to say that, whether we contemplate the manufacturers of Manchester as masters having the common feelings of humanity towards their workpeople, or as commercial men possessing an intelligent appreciation of the springs of commercial prosperity; it is equally their duty and their interest to undertake this labour of buying and contracting for cotton on the spot where it grows. This policy of waiting with folded arms until something shall happen to make things right again is not the policy by which the industrial greatness of this country was built up. The Cotton Lords have been for many years a plutocracy. All things have been made smooth for them, and everything has gone down before them. The one thing they have given us in return is employment in comfort, and high wages, to many thousands of English families." The article also attacks Richard Cobden for "his zeal and his anger and his almost feminine rage." ("The

The Cotton Famine: Shop for mill hands at Birley's Mill

Times", 1st August 1862.)
2) This situation was strongly disapproved of by another frequent visitor to Manchester, Karl Marx. He hoped that the widespread distress would cause the impoverished operatives to rise in revolt. However, when this failed to materialise, he referred in a letter to Engels to the "damaging" effect of "the sheep-like behaviour of the Lancashire workers. Such a thing has never been heard of in the world." (Marx/Engels, "Werke" (Berlin 1974), XXX, 301.)
3) Adams' account of Manchester was written in the early days of the Cotton Famine when the crisis had not really begun to bite. Compare Adams' view here with that of a German journalist who visited Manchester in 1865 whilst on his way to Rochdale to write a report on the co-operatives there. "It was not a favourable time to get to know the busy city, the city which sends its products to Siberia and Africa, which delivers material for clothes to the Chinese in their tea gardens and to the red Indian squaws in their rocky mountains. The tense pressure of the cotton crisis (or cotton famine, as the English say) hung over the city and country. Many factories stood still and their gigantic chimneys rose, ghostly and inactive, into the unusually clear air; the streets and squares - even the usually lively ones in the city centre - were relatively quiet... idle workers were standing in groups at the street corners talking about the times of hardship and the latest news from America." ("Daheim", Jahrgang I (1865), pp344-345, Staatsarchiv Bielefeld.)

Ellen Barlee
(fl 1862)

Another visitor attracted by the crisis of the cotton famine in Manchester was Ellen Barlee. She paid particular attention to the various relief funds and organisations and also to the several sewing schools in the town.

"On my first visiting Manchester in company with a friend, my impression of the aspect of the city, in reference to the cotton famine, was, that had I not previously known that the inhabitants were suffering from privation, I should never have guessed that any unusual cloud hung over the place. As we walked down the streets, no crowds of idlers, no whining beggars, no groups of factory girls, were to be seen; nor was there any unusual excitement anywhere to remind us that the greater part of the labouring population were out of work. Indeed, I feel convinced that any foreigner unacquainted with the convulsion of the cotton trade might visit Manchester without having his curiosity aroused on the subject. On inquiry, however, we found that the quiet deportment of the place was occasioned by the many institutions at work to provide for the unemployed. Manchester on this point is better off than many other towns. It has more wealthy inhabitants residing in and near it - fewer mill operatives in proportion to its population; whilst the number of professional poor that congregate in every large city, and infest the streets or live upon beggary, are now benefitting by the grants made by the Relief Committees to all indigent persons, and are better off than they ever were before.

The effect of the cotton famine is therefore less felt here than elsewhere; still, the official authorities, and the various agents of the many voluntary charities at work for the poor, have their hands quite full; and we were much interested in following the round of such schemes as were in operation for the relief of distress...

Every applicant for relief has to attend the office of the district in which he resides, and lodge his complaints before the committee there. An officer is then sent to investigate his claim, and, if found correct, the grant is accorded him. At Manchester, as well as every other place I visited, the most stringent rules are enforced to prevent imposition; the recipient of public bounty being obliged to lay bare his circumstances, and mention every available source of income he receives. This demand is carried to such an extent, that should an individual receive even a few shillings in private charity, he is expected to report the gift, and, in most cases, it is deducted from the allowance awarded him...

The Provident Society... from the commencement of the cotton famine has been actively employed in alleviating distress. The operations are carried on in an old mill, with about as wretched an entrance as can well be imagined. Groups of professional beggars and squalid poor were seen hanging about the door...

The rickety old mill where the Provident Society holds its office forms a capital place for the administration of relief. We were conducted all over it, and found each room was set apart for some work in connexion with the cotton distress. In one was a sewing class for 200 girls; in another a soup cooking apparatus, to feed them; in a third, blankets and clothing were stored; a fourth, which... was fitted up with barricades or pens, and looking like a miniature cattle market, was the room in which the applicants came to receive relief, either in money or kind. The barricades were placed to avoid a crush, as from the numbers there would be danger of injury. Everything seemed planned with the greatest method...

Before we left the place our sympathies were fully called out in behalf of a class hitherto overlooked... I allude to the numerous clerks, warehouse men and salesmen of once thriving Manchester, who, thrown out of employment by the commercial stagnation of the times, are with their families reduced to utter destitution. Till quite lately the tide of benevolence which rose so liberally to the cry of the distressed operatives has passed by these men in its flow, and alone, unregarded, they have fought perhaps a harder battle with want than anyone knows, or of any other persons in the place...

Before quitting Manchester, the last day of my visit we went over the central clothing depot, and a curious sight enough it was to see the... apparel that had been forwarded there from all parts of the Kingdom. When the bales arrive they are deposited in one room, where they are opened as soon as possible and the contents sorted into different heaps. Petticoats, bonnets, blankets, boots and shoes, with dresses of all kinds, are arranged in a marvellous medley, both of character and kind. The well worn and the scarcely soiled, the useful and the ornamental, are mixed up together; whilst I could but notice a scarlet hunting coat... lying side by side with the fustian and other more suitable suits of men's clothing. Everybody, however, has contributed their quota, and a visit to the various clothing depots helps to form no bad idea of the widespread sympathy and liberal spirit which pervade all classes...

In the warehouse of the Manchester depot, strung across the room, suspended from the ceiling, and above heaps of clothing, we were astonished to see joints of meat, venison, game, bacon, etc... we were informed that they were gifts sent to the central depot for the operatives."

Barlee concluded her observations of Manchester with the hope that "Lancashire men and women may come forth from their trial, though, maybe a saddened, yet a wiser and more God-fearing people."

Notes
The text is from E Barlee, "A Visit to Lancashire in December 1862" (1863), pp69-102.

Index of Visitors

Henry Adams	60f
Ellen Barlee	61f
John Britton	23
Eugene Buret	5,35f
Johann Büsch	14
John Byng	19f
William Camden	3,9f
Karl Carus	34,35
W R Chambers	54ff
Henry Colman	42f
Samuel Curwen	9,13f
"Daheim" (report from)	61
Daniel Defoe	3,10,11f
Charles Dibdin	20
Charles Dickens	5
Friedrich Engels	3,5,6,35,37ff 46,47,49
Johann Escher	25ff
Leon Faucher	43ff
Johann Ferbers	6
Celia Fiennis	3,10
Johann Fischer	28
Don Manuel Gonzales	10,11
Julian Harney	7
Nathaniel Hawthorne	3
Johann Hogrewe	14,15ff,17
John Horsley	3,11
Victor Huber	4,35
The Chevalier de Johnstone	13
Johann Kohl	49ff
John Leland	3,8f,9
Wilhelm Lenssen	3,32
Johann May	25
Johann Meidinger	17,30ff
Gustav von Mevissen	5
Fynes Moryson	9,10
Charles Napier	5
Philip Nemnich	4,21ff
William Nicholson	12
William Philips	20f
Friedrich von Raumer	34
James Ray	12f
Karl Schinkel	28
Johanna Schopenhauer	28f
Robert Southey	6,24
William Stukeley	3,10f
Friedrich von Tauber	17,18,19
William Taylor	6,36f
Times journalist (1862)	61
Alexis de Tocqueville	32f
Jakob Venedey	46ff
Queen Victoria	58ff
Ludwig von Vincke	21
Johann Volkmann	17ff
Rev Richard Warner	3,4
Arthur Young	17

****

For a current list of local history publications available by post, please send a stamped addressed envelope to Neil Richardson, 88 Ringley Road, Stoneclough, Radcliffe, Manchester M26 1ET
****